PICKING UP THE Pᵢ

Picking Up The Pieces *provides a forensic analysis of where Ireland went wrong and what we need to do to rebuild the economy. Jim Power outlines the folly of allowing unelected social partners to run the country. The decline in competitiveness, the inability to say 'no' to vested interest groups and the unsustainability of construction activity are all at the heart of our economic demise.*

Jim points the way to economic recovery through cost reductions in wages, commercial rents and rates and professional fees. He charts a course to improve our communications capability, labour force quality and physical infrastructure. The book pinpoints the growth potential of FDI, tourism, agri-food, green energy, the arts and professional services. Above all, he argues, we need visionary leadership rather than populist politics. This book is a must-read for all concerned about our current economic woes.

Ivan Yates, presenter on Newstalk 106–108
and former Fine Gael TD

Jim Power pulls no punches when it comes to apportioning blame for the squandered opportunities of the Celtic Tiger boom. This authoritative book serves up the facts and figures in a jargon-free way, highlighting the shortcomings, extracting the lessons and illuminating the path to recovery in a concise and eminently readable manner.

Mark Fielding, Chief Executive, ISME

Jim Power has written an important book describing the rise and fall of the Celtic Tiger. The analysis is presented in clear, jargon-free English – economists will hate it. Jim convincingly makes the case that Ireland has fallen into the time-honoured trap of allowing the commanding heights of the economy to be captured by vested interests and political elites. Global economic history is full of similar examples – the US and Argentina used to have exactly the same GDP per capita until the Argentinian elite forced the economy to serve its, rather than the wider, interest. The rest is history. Ireland risks a similar fate unless our elites change course. Jim lays out what those policies should be.

Chris Johns, Head of Investments,
Bank of Ireland Asset Management

Picking Up The Pieces

Economic Crisis and Hope in Ireland

Jim Power

BLACKHALL
Publishing

Published by

Blackhall Publishing
Lonsdale House
Avoca Avenue
Blackrock
Co. Dublin
Ireland

e-mail: info@blackhallpublishing.com
www.blackhallpublishing.com

© Jim Power, 2009

ISBN: 978-1-84218-183-6

Printed in the Republic of Ireland by ColourBooks Ltd.

For Anne, Robert, Conor and my mother, Della

Jim Power is a well-known economic commentator and is currently chief economist with Friends First. He has a regular column in the *Irish Examiner* and also writes for other publications. He is a frequent commentator on radio and TV and he lectures on the MBA programme in DCU Business School and the UCD Michael Smurfit Graduate Business School.

Preface

I wrote this book out of a deep sense of anger and frustration at the manner in which the Irish economy and Irish society have been directed in recent years.

Unfortunately, much of what has passed for economic prosperity over the past decade was built on foundations of debt, and that is never a sustainable situation. The economy and, indeed, the country are now in a mess and our politicians do not appear to have the vision, ability or leadership qualities to extricate us from it. This is not acceptable. We cannot stand back and accept defeat in the manner that we now appear to be doing. Neither can we stand back and wait in the vain hope that our political system will solve the crisis. Many people care passionately about the future of Ireland, and so they should. We cannot allow a situation to develop whereby our brightest and best young people become the country's biggest export. We also cannot allow ourselves to pass on a legacy of government debt and poor quality public services such as health and education to the next generation.

There is no silver-bullet solution to Ireland's current difficulties, but neither will it take rocket science. To my way of thinking, the policy platform we need to create is blindingly obvious, but there is no desire to grasp the nettle. The renewed Programme for Government agreed between Fianna Fáil and the Green Party in the early days of October

2009 does not fill me with any sense of confidence that the right decisions will be taken. It is time for those who have the best interests of the country at heart to force our flawed political establishment to do the right thing.

I decided to write this book after Bertie Ahern stood down as taoiseach in 2008 because I passionately believed – and still do – that his economic legacy was not what he and his supporters made it out to be. I wanted to call the book *Bertie, It Could Have Been So Much Better*, but later thought that a more forward-looking and hopeful title such as *Picking Up The Pieces* would be more appropriate. However, I retain a firm conviction that, but for the nature of the political and economic leadership since 1997, Ireland's problems today would not be as deep or as long term. I have sought to explore this theme throughout the book.

I would like to sincerely thank my editor at Blackhall Publishing, Elizabeth Brennan, for her skill, patience, good humour and forbearance in getting this book to publication stage. I would also like to thank my good friend Chris Johns for his helpful comments. Finally, I thank my wife and two sons for their patience over recent months.

My key motivation for writing this book was to contribute to a constructive debate that might ultimately sow the seeds for the development of a country where my two boys will be able to make a decent life, should they so desire. That looks far from guaranteed at the moment, but we must live in hope.

Jim Power
October 2009

Contents

Introduction

Standing next to me in this lonely crowd,
Is a man who swears he's not to blame.
All day long I hear him shout so loud,
Crying out that he was framed.
                    Bob Dylan, 'I Shall Be Released', 1967

Economists are frequently berated over their inability to forecast the future with any degree of accuracy. How often do we
hear people argue that the economics profession failed
abysmally to anticipate the imminent collapse of the Irish
economy in recent years? There is an old joke to the effect
that economic forecasting was invented to make weather
forecasting look good. Indeed, in some quarters, economists
are being blamed for much of what has happened in the
economy. Those who work for vested interest groups such as
banks or estate agents are frequently picked out for special
attention and are accused of fanning the flames that eventually burned up the Irish economy.

The last couple of years have been particularly difficult for
economic forecasters given the unprecedented nature of the
global economic shock. Even the vast majority of those who
were generally sceptical about the direction in which the
Irish economy was being driven in recent years failed to fully
anticipate the extent of the downturn that has now occurred
and the damage that has been done to the banking system. Of
course, the reality is that the global economy has experienced

1

a once-in-a-century event and Ireland's fragile economic model has been savagely exposed. Also, during apparently good economic times nobody was particularly interested in hearing bad news. Over the past couple of years I have literally spoken at hundreds of different events in many parts of Ireland. I could count on one hand the number of these events at which I was not asked to be as upbeat as possible and to try to view the glass as being half full rather than half empty. My stock reply to such requests is that I do not seek to view the glass as either half full or half empty, but simply as it is. It is incumbent on any economist or commentator to be as honest as possible and paint as true a picture as possible. I have always tried to adopt this approach and on many occasions I have been wrong, but hopefully I have been right more than 50 per cent of the time.

The problem with economic forecasting is that economics is not an exact science, putting it mildly. With a physical science such as chemistry it is possible to put two elements into a test tube and get a certain outcome. With a social science like economics, outcomes are not determined by an exact and predictable process, but rather are determined by the actions and reactions of ordinary people, business people and politicians to different circumstances and events. In other words, it is subject to the vagaries of human behaviour, and there is, in my experience, nothing more unpredictable than human behaviour. Geopolitical events such as 9/11 will inevitably have a huge economic impact that no economic model can properly predict or capture. Likewise, when bankers behave badly, as they did to incredible effect in the US subprime mortgage market, or indeed here in Ireland in relation to lending to developers, it is difficult to capture it fully in an economic forecast, not least because we have incomplete information and have to rely heavily on what the bankers themselves are telling us. We have discovered over the past couple of years that the guidance we received from the banks was deeply flawed. Likewise, economic outcomes are very often determined by political developments and, in the real world of politics, what makes economic sense does not

2

always make political sense, so it is not always wise to apply economic logic to the economic policies implemented by politicians. Perhaps the most difficult effect to measure in an economic forecast is that of madness of crowds. When people get caught up in a bubble mania, logic goes out the window and economic forecasts become pretty meaningless and irrelevant. The performance of the Irish housing market in the first half of 2006 is a good example of this phenomenon.

Any economist or commentator who is arrogant enough to believe that theirs is the only view worth listening to is delusional. Likewise, it is dangerous to take the forecasts of an economist, or indeed of anybody, as written in stone. The truth is that the future can never be forecast with absolute certainty, but economic analysis does provide the tools for identifying risks and trying to guard against them. The managers of the Irish economy have not done this very successfully over the past decade.

An embarrassing problem for economic forecasters is that forecasts generally go into the public record and, thanks to the Internet, the legacy can survive for years and will inevitably come back to haunt you at some later date. When researching this book, I did a Google search for an article I had written some years ago and was taken aback at the manner in which things I have written over the years are used by anonymous participants in chat rooms to be as insulting as possible. However, that is life, and if you comment publicly on issues, then you open yourself up to such criticism and insult. I came in for special mention by UCD sociologist Kieran Allen[1] in June 2009. He extracted a forecast of mine dating back a couple of years, which would not exactly have won me a Nobel Prize in economics, but which was also not one of the worst forecasts I ever made. If he had done a bit more research he would have been able to do me much more damage, if that was his intention.

While economic forecasting is a hazardous business, the business of life in Ireland has also become hazardous in recent times. As Chapter 1 outlines, Ireland is now in a difficult and uncertain place and it is not at all clear how and when the economy will emerge from its morass. The national spirit has been seriously dampened and the sense of optimism that has prevailed for the past decade or more has dissipated with alarming rapidity. The stark human face of this economic and financial tragedy is still unfolding. Thousands have lost their pensions and their jobs and thousands more are living in houses the values of which have fallen below the level of their mortgages. The college graduates of 2009 would not appear to have too many options, and even the traditional escape valve of emigration has been at least temporarily blocked as a result of the global economic and financial crisis unleashed by the greed and stupidity of global bankers and policy-makers.

I visit the United States on a regular basis and always return to Ireland with a sense of enthusiasm and a real can-do attitude. However, when I came back into the country towards the end of summer 2009, all I could feel was a sense of disillusionment and frustration. The debate was still going on about the National Asset Management Agency (NAMA), the *Commission on Taxation Report* and the *Report of the Special Group on Public Service Numbers and Expenditure Programmes* on cutting public expenditure. It appears that we have been arguing about these issues for the best part of the past year and we still haven't reached a conclusion or indeed agreement on what needs to be done. Such prevarication is very frustrating and damaging for individuals and businesses who just want to get on with it.

The mood of the Irish population today ranges from anger to despondency. The worrying question is that if the many problems in Irish society were not sorted out in times of plenty, what chance is there now? There is a sense of disbelief that the situation could have altered so dramatically and so suddenly. Many people now finally realise that much of the Irish economic edifice was built on foundations of debt and greed. The chickens have come home to roost and the country is possibly facing the most immense challenges since independence.

Of course, this sense of crisis is not new for Ireland; we are basically just back to where we were in the 1980s. As Chapter 2 explains, at that stage the economy was in a mess, the public finances were in very serious deficit and people represented the biggest category of export from the country. This exporting of young people drained the country of hope and brainpower, and seriously undermined the economic and social potential of the economy. The lesson from the 1980s is that a combination of external influences, not least the IMF lurking in the background, forced real political leadership to the surface. The political system eventually responded and sensible policies combined with favourable external developments and some luck to propel Ireland on to a higher growth plane that was to eventually lead to the period of prosperity known as the Celtic Tiger. Ireland had innovated itself from the brink of disaster to the pinnacle of global economic performance, or so it appeared. High levels of economic growth became the norm. Happy days! While economic growth continued at very strong levels up to 2007, the nature of the growth was changing.

The notion had developed at the peak of the Celtic Tiger that Ireland had become a self-sustaining economic entity that could survive on its citizens building houses for each other and buying goods and services from each other. It was even better that we were in a position to start bringing in people from overseas to build even more houses for each other, and Government was more than happy to go along with the charade because it put a very healthy complexion on the overall economy and spawned billions in tax revenues.

The model of Ireland as a small open economy where exports are the lifeblood of economic activity was forgotten and neglected. Ireland became fat and arrogant and we allowed the cost base of the country to get totally out of control, and with it the general competitiveness of the country. Unfortunately, but perhaps inevitably, the new model based on house building and consumer spending came to a shuddering halt in 2007 due to a variety of factors, and the Irish

5

economy was pushed into the deepest recession in its history by 2009.

Policy-makers, and indeed the rest of us, became totally caught up in the booming economy. Unfortunately, very few with influence actually stood back and questioned if the emerging trends in the economy were actually sustainable. If they had, the answer would be no. The whole focus was on quantity in terms of the number of jobs being created and the level of economic growth. The quality and sustainability of the economic and employment growth was never considered and the country is now paying a heavy price for that lack of vision.

Chapters 3 to 6 describe the web of policy-making that led to Ireland moving to such an unsustainable position. Bertie Ahern's successive governments allowed the Irish economy to become inordinately dependent on the construction sector, which became the biggest driver of tax revenues, employment, the Irish equity market and general economic activity. This, along with the Government's general economic illiteracy, mismanagement of public finances, flawed fiscal policy, pandering to vested interest groups and inability to make tough decisions led to Ireland's current heightened vulnerability. The country is currently trying to cope with a global recession on top of the dramatic bursting of a housing bubble with all of its consequent travails. However, I don't intend to launch into a rant about what went wrong in this book. Rather, I want to identify the mistakes of the past ten years as the first step to rectifying them.

The sad and annoying fact is that we can be sure that before the whole process of cleaning up the discredited banking system will have run its course, it will have cost the Irish taxpayer an awful lot of money. Future generations will be paying the bill directly or indirectly for years to come. The other harsh reality is that, from being the darling of Europe and the world just a couple of years ago, Ireland has become a source of embarrassment to people who care about the country. Our international reputation has been seriously tarnished.

From a social and economic perspective, Ireland simply cannot afford another brain drain of the type that devastated Irish society and the economy in the 1980s. It is incumbent on our policy-makers to show courage and vision in addressing the problems facing the country. To date, that courage and vision has not been too obvious.

Ireland is not a large country and in many ways it is akin to a large US corporation. It should not take a group of rocket scientists to figure out what needs to be done and, more importantly, to ensure that it is done. Chapters 7 and 8 deal with the conditions and policies necessary for Ireland to recover. In the short-term the competitiveness of the economy needs to be restored, the crisis in the banking system has to be sorted out, and the structural imbalances in the public finances need to be rectified. In the longer term, Ireland's policy-makers should develop a strategic vision of what type of economy and society they want to generate, and the citizens of the country need to get actively involved in creating this vision and making sure it is delivered. Active participation by the citizenry is now required to shape the future because the political system and the structures of the state have failed us badly, and it is not at all clear that, as currently constituted, they have the ability to take Ireland out of its dire situation.

This book not only seeks to chart how we got into this current crisis but also to recommend what needs to be done to get us out of it. The important point is that the task is not impossible, but requires vision, leadership and a level of strategic insight that has been lacking in the political and state system in recent years. Those who contributed to the current economic and financial mess must be held accountable and cannot be allowed back into positions of influence ever again. The system needs to be cleansed because the only way that the population can possibly accept the inevitable pain over the coming years is if those responsible are held accountable. Unfortunately, there is not a strong precedent for such accountability in Irish business or politics. That needs to change.

There are still many individuals and companies operating in the Irish economy who believe in the future of the country and who will continue to try to make it happen. The challenge for policy-makers is to create an environment where such individuals and companies are facilitated to the greatest extent possible in order to create high quality economic activity and employment, and help Ireland realise its economic potential in a manner that can be sustained. The bottom line is that there is no easy solution to this crisis and there is no painless way out of it. Hopefully, as happened in the 1980s, true leadership will emerge.

If there is one thing I really want to contribute with this book, it is to demonstrate the folly of populist political decision making, which was *the* key feature of the Ahern era, and also to show that, when vested interest groups take control of the policy-making process, necessary change is prevented. Okay, so that's two things. But I'm an economist so I can change my mind.

Ultimately, unless we examine our past and learn from it, history just has a nasty habit of repeating itself.

1

The State of the Nation in 2009

*Ireland is being forced to raise taxes and slash govern-
ment spending in the face of an economic slump –
policies that will further deepen the slump.*
Paul Krugman, *New York Times*, 19 April 2009

The Depression of 2009 and the Political Fallout

The year 2009 will be remembered in Ireland with mixed
emotions. It saw the definitive end of a prolonged period of
unprecedented and uninterrupted economic growth and
prosperity. It was also the year in which Ireland's semi-
permanent government party, Fianna Fáil, slipped to third
place in the political pecking order on the basis of opinion
polls, and subsequently got whacked in the European and
local elections. While there was a certain inevitability about
the demise of the economy – no economy can escape the realities of the economic cycle forever – the dramatic opinion poll
collapse in support for Fianna Fáil in the run up to the local
and European elections in June 2009, and the corresponding
fall in the party's vote in the actual elections, did come as a
bigger shock to many. The notoriously populist Fianna Fáil
party has always been a venerable part of Irish life, and to see
public opinion turn so dramatically against it does represent
a momentous development.

Perhaps the demise of the party should not have come as
such a surprise because Fianna Fáil-led governments since
1997 helped lay the basis for the destruction of the economy

that occurred in 2008 and 2009. On the other hand, it has been proven time and time again over the years that the hardcore supporters of Fianna Fáil continually vote for that party regardless of how it behaves in terms of economic management or basic probity. It was once suggested to me that if Fianna Fáil ran a donkey in an election in Clare it would get elected. Indeed, one could argue that the party has had many donkeys elected in many parts of the country over the years, but that might be a bit cruel. Nevertheless, seeing Irish voters turning against Fianna Fáil is not something that we are accustomed to in Ireland.

The actual election results in June 2009 were quite devastating for what has traditionally been Ireland's biggest party. Fine Gael recorded its first ever election victory over Fianna Fáil in a national election and won a greater share of the vote in both elections. In the local elections, Fine Gael won 32.3 per cent of first preference votes compared to 24.4 per cent for its biggest political rival. In the European elections, Fine Gael won 29.1 per cent of first preference votes compared to 24 per cent for Fianna Fáil. Only time will tell if these election results mark a permanent change in the nature of Irish politics, but, even if they don't, they still represent a seismic event in Irish political and social life.

The background to this extraordinary political turnaround is not too difficult to understand. During his first year as taoiseach, Brian Cowen's popularity took a serious battering in the face of an unprecedented economic crisis and Cowen became one of the most unpopular leaders in Irish political history. As the economy plummeted in 2008–2009, Cowen and his senior ministers were akin to the proverbial rabbit caught in the headlights. Arguably, their biggest mistake – and that of their predecessors – was the failure to face up to the reality of the economic crisis that began to evolve in 2007. By the time they started to react in anything resembling a decisive manner, it was already too late. Indeed, over the years, members of the Government were quite disparaging and dismissive of those who dared to criticise the economy. There is a tendency amongst Irish politicians to brand anybody who dares criticise their party or their policies as a 'Blueshirt', a 'Fianna Failer', a 'left-wing pinko'or some other derisory term.

As I examine later in this chapter, when the Government did eventually recognise the gravity of the evolving crisis, they failed to act decisively and appropriately. For example, the Budget of October 2008 certainly did not reflect the gravity of the situation, the public sector pension levy in February 2009 was misguided, and the heavy bias towards higher personal taxes in the Supplementary Budget of April 2009 was not in my view the most appropriate policy response to a deepening economic recession, but was consistent with most of what went before.

In the aftermath of the election, various members of the government parties expressed the view that they had been punished for the hard decisions that they had taken over the preceding year, but that ultimately these decisions would work in the best interests of the economy. This is a strange and misguided interpretation. The truth is that, as well as being blamed for the policies that in large part led to the deepening economic crisis, the government parties were punished for what they had failed to do rather than for what they had done in the face of it; they were punished for inactivity rather than activity. The Irish electorate had arguably reached the stage where it would have welcomed decisive and tough measures to address the crisis, but instead it got prevarication and cowardice, and it punished accordingly.

Perhaps the electorate also couldn't ignore the fact that earlier incarnations of the incumbent Government allowed an insane property bubble to develop and, through various ill-informed policies, ensured that the economy was increasingly forced to fly on one wing – property. That wing was decisively broken off during 2008 and the economic and financial consequences proved quite devastating.

The reaction of Government to the crisis was pretty feeble because they either did not recognise the gravity of the problem or lacked the political will and confidence to do anything about it. It was probably a combination of both. Most members of the Government had become so accustomed to giving the electorate everything that they asked for and more, that the notion of making hard decisions to try to get the rapidly deteriorating public finances back on track was totally alien to their very nature. Unfortunately, it is very difficult for any government reared on populist policy-making to turn around and behave sensibly when circumstances call for such a response.

The State of the Nation in 2009

The state of the Irish nation in 2008 was not good, to put it mildly, and became a lot worse in 2009. Following average annual growth of 7.2 per cent in gross domestic product (GDP)* between 1997 and 2007 and annual average growth of 6.3 per cent in gross national product (GNP), economic activity weakened sharply as 2008 progressed. In the final quarter of 2008, GDP recorded an annual contraction of 8 per cent and GNP contracted by 7.2 per cent. For 2008 as a whole, GDP fell by 3 per cent and GNP by 2.8 per cent.[1] This was the first annual contraction in economic activity since 1983 and marked a major turning point in Ireland's recent economic history.

Unfortunately the contraction in activity in 2008 was only the tip of the iceberg and, as 2009 progressed, it became increasingly and painfully clear that the party had really ended and that the economic nightmare had definitely begun. Indeed, as the economy descended into the deepest growth recession in many decades in the early months of 2009, there was a growing sense that the situation was getting out of control. In the first quarter of 2009, GDP contracted by 9.3 per

*Gross Domestic Product (GDP) is the total value of goods and services produced in an economy in a given time period. Some of the factors of production used to produce GDP are not owned by Irish residents, so some of the income accruing to foreign-owned factors of production finds its way out of the country to the foreign owners. These flows are called net factor flows. When GDP is adjusted for those factor flows, we are left with Gross National Product (GNP). In Ireland in 2008, GNP was €27 billion lower than GDP, largely due to the reparation of profits by foreign multinationals operating in Ireland.

cent and GNP by a massive 13.1 per cent. This effectively meant that, in the first quarter of 2009, almost 10 cent had been removed from every euro of national income that was generated in 2008. This was the largest ever recorded decline in national income in Ireland and conveyed the strong impression that the economy had pretty much gone into free fall. Consumer spending in the first three months of 2009 was almost 10 per cent lower than a year earlier and investment collapsed by a massive 34 per cent.[2] This was dramatic by any standards. In the second quarter of 2009, GDP contracted by 7.4 per cent and GNP by 11.6 per cent, suggesting some stabilisation.

In line with this economic collapse, Ireland's international standing took a serious battering. The three main rating agencies in the global financial system – Moody's, Standard & Poor's and Fitch – all downgraded Ireland's international credit rating; at the time of writing, Standard & Poor's had actually already downgraded us twice. The rating agencies basically attach a risk assessment to debt issued by countries or companies and this assessment is a key determinant of the interest rate that a country or company has to pay to lenders. When investors invest in the debt of a company or a country, they generally seek to get a return that will cover anticipated inflation over the period of their loan in order to preserve the real purchasing power of their money, but they also seek to be rewarded for taking on the risk that the borrower might default. The riskier a country or a company is deemed to be, the greater the risk premium that lenders will seek to achieve. The rating attached to the debt of a company or a country seeks to measure that risk.

While the agencies have suffered a serious loss of credibility themselves over the past couple of years as a result of their failure to properly assess the risk attaching to international investment products that were based on subprime mortgages, they are still listened to by investors. The practical implication of this is very real and tangible – Ireland now has to pay 2 per cent more than Germany to borrow money, and unfortunately the country will have to borrow an awful lot of money over the next few years to finance the spiralling borrowing requirement. In a monetary union, it would not be usual for a country to have to pay a higher interest rate premium than fellow members, given that there is no exchange rate risk involved, but the manner in which the Irish economy and its financial system has imploded over the past couple of years has ensured that the country has become a much more risky proposition for international investors. The good news is that the differential was much wider earlier in 2009, so at least international investors are becoming more relaxed. This is somewhat encouraging.

In understanding why the economy experienced such a sudden and sharp reversal of fortunes we need look no further than the housing market.

In 2006, the construction industry delivered 93,419 new housing units, representing an all-time annual record. Completions in 2008 totalled 51,724[3] and, based on activity levels in 2009, completions are likely to fall to no more than 20,000 units. My expectation is that less than 15,000 houses will be built in 2010. The construction boom has truly ended and this is exacting a heavy price on an economy that had become totally intoxicated by property. Statistically, we know that for every 10,000 fewer new houses built, around 1.2 per cent is pared off the economic growth rate. Building a new house creates direct construction industry employment, injects wages into the economy, results in the purchase of building materials, furniture and fittings following completion, creates a demand for auctioneering and legal services, and makes a major contribution to Exchequer tax revenues.

By 2006, housing activity had become the key driver of tax revenues, employment creation and overall economic activity. Consequently, the sharp correction in the housing market since 2007 is the key explanatory variable in the recent dramatic demise of the Irish economy.

In many ways this reversal in the fortunes of the housing market was not undesirable because the economy had become dangerously dependent on housing activity; house prices had attained levels that undermined competitiveness and created a serious vulnerability. As house prices increased, borrowers were forced to take on bigger mortgages, and in turn sought higher wages to service the bigger mortgages, which helped undermine the cost competitiveness of the economy. Unfortunately, what started out as a desirable construction sector adjustment in 2007 very quickly spread across other sectors of the economy. By the mid-point of 2009, almost every sector of the economy had become weak, and business and consumer confidence had hit historic lows.

However desirable such a housing market correction might be, it was always going to be a painful adjustment experience for the overall economy, but the pain was exacerbated by the collapse in global economic activity. For a small open economy like Ireland, where the value of exports and imports of goods and services account for over 150 per cent of GDP[4] (the equivalent in the US is just over 30 per cent[5]), a deterioration in the global economy was always going to cause serious economic problems. The very difficult external economic environment was caused by the implosion of the US subprime mortgage market, which commenced in the middle of 2007 and spread during 2008 and into 2009. This implosion undoubtedly represents the greatest financial and economic shock experienced by the global economy since the 1930s and global economic activity was plunged into the sharpest correction since the Second World War.

So, for Ireland, a painful housing market adjustment was made a lot worse by the most difficult set of external circumstances in decades, and the economy fell into crisis. The following snapshot of economic data from 2009, relating to a number of key areas, gives a stark picture of the dramatic collapse of the economy and highlights the immense challenges facing the Government.

Government Finances

The Exchequer returns for the first nine months of 2009 showed that the Government ran a financial deficit of €20.1

billion. This compares to a deficit of €9.4 billion for the same period in 2008. At the end of September 2009, tax revenues were running 16.8 per cent behind the first nine months of 2008. Stamp duties were running 50 per cent behind those for 2008, which in turn were well behind the previous year. This reflects the reduction in housing transactions. VAT receipts were down by 21.3 per cent, indicating weak consumer spending and the collapse in new house building. Income tax receipts were running 9.4 per cent behind 2008, despite the various levies that had been introduced since the first attempt at a recession budget in October 2008. Corporation tax was 22.6 per cent ahead of 2008, but this reflected changes to the timing of corporation tax payments. The underlying situation was weak, mirroring the ongoing pressure on profitability across the corporate sector, but particularly in financial services. Finally, capital gains tax receipts were running 68.4 per cent[6] behind those of 2008, which is no surprise given that very few capital gains have been made over the past couple of years; now most Irish investors would not recognise a capital gain if it jumped up and bit them in the face. The bottom line is that the collapse in tax revenues as a result of weaker economic activity and the upward pressure on government spending as a result of spiralling unemployment caused the public finances to deteriorate in an alarming manner and has created a serious fiscal crisis for the Government.

Employment

Employment data for the second quarter of 2009 show that employment fell by 27,100 during the quarter, and fell by 174,300 compared to the same quarter in 2008. Over the twelve-month period, the private sector shed 190,400 jobs, while the public sector created 16,100 jobs. On the unemployment front, the number of people signing on to the live register increased to 429,400 on a seasonally adjusted basis in September 2009. This represents an increase of 263,400 since September 2007. The unemployment rate jumped from 4.5 per cent of the labour force in the middle of 2007 to 12.6 per cent in September 2009.[7] The live register is not designed to measure unemployment as it includes part-time workers, defined as those who work up to three days per week, and seasonal and casual workers entitled to Jobseeker's Benefit or Allowance. However, the live register is still a pretty good reflection of what is going on in the labour market, and the message it conveyed about the labour market in 2009 was not good. But for renewed outward migration, the live register situation would have been considerably worse.

Wealth

Figures released by the Central Statistics Office (CSO) show that the net financial assets of the household and non-profit institutions sector fell by €36 billion during 2008 to €81.2 billion. Net financial assets describes the difference between deposits, shares, life insurance and pension fund assets on one side of the personal balance sheet, and mainly loans on the other side. Over the two years 2007 and 2008, the cumulative decline was €58.7 billion, representing a decline of 42 per cent since the highest recorded level of net assets – worth €139.9 billion at the end of 2006. The key contributory factor to this decline in wealth during 2008 was the sharp decline in share prices, pension funds and insurance. A point worth noting is that the value of housing wealth is not included in this calculation, so the real destruction of personal wealth was even more dramatic in 2007 and 2008 than the official data suggests.

Retail Sales

Given the level of personal wealth destruction, it is no surprise that consumer spending has dropped dramatically. The volume of retail sales in the first eight months of 2009 was 16.6 per cent lower than in the first eight months of 2008. This slowdown in retail spending reflected the pressure on disposable incomes from falling employment, nominal wage cuts in many sectors of the economy and the increased personal tax burden inherent in the Government's fiscal consolidation strategy. In addition, as mentioned, there has been considerable destruction of personal wealth over the past couple of years. The key weakness in retail sales is in the auto sector. Excluding the motor trade, retail sales were 7.1 per cent lower in the first eight months of 2009 compared to the same period in 2008.[8] Car sales took an awful hammering in 2008 and 2009, and many long-established car dealers were forced out of business. After years of rampant growth in consumer spending, an adjustment of this magnitude is pretty dramatic and is suggestive of a consumer whose animal spirits have been seriously dampened.

Manufacturing Activity

Manufacturing output in the first eight months of 2009 was 2 per cent lower than in the first eight months of 2008. Output from the 'modern sector' was up by 5.9 per cent, while output from the 'traditional sector' was down by 14.7 per cent.[9] The modern sector comprises a number of high-technology, chemical and pharmaceutical companies that are predominately foreign-owned. The traditional sector takes in the rest; it includes sectors such as food and beverages, textiles, and furniture. Clearly there is a serious dichotomy in Irish manufacturing activity. The gap is continuing to widen, which has to be a matter of longer-term concern for the economy.

Inflation

On the back of weaker demand in the economy and the sharp fall in mortgage interest rates, consumer price inflation declined rapidly in the first nine months of 2009. The headline rate of inflation in September showed an annual decline of 6.5 per cent. Excluding mortgage rates, prices declined by 2.4 per cent in the year to September.[10] This decline in prices is positive, because it shows that the cost of living in the economy is adjusting to the changed economic realities, just as private sector wages are adjusting. After a number of years during which Ireland's cost competitiveness was undermined by inflation rates well in excess of our main trading partners,

18

the downward adjustment in prices does represent good news. However, it is not an unambiguously positive picture because prices are still rising strongly in sheltered parts of the economy, such as health, education, child care and insurance. The big challenge for the authorities is to try and ensure that prices across the whole economy adjust in a downward direction, in order to alleviate upward pressure on wages and social welfare payments and restore cost competitiveness.

The above statistics clearly demonstrate the very difficult economic situation in the first half of 2009. Unfortunately, few forecasters are holding out too much hope for a meaningful economic recovery in the foreseeable future. The International Monetary Fund (IMF) forecasted that Ireland's GDP would contract by 8.5 per cent in 2009 and by 3 per cent in 2010.[11] This would imply a contraction of 13.5 per cent in the size of the Irish economy in the three-year period to 2010. A decline of more than 10 per cent is technically defined as a depression. Furthermore, a decline of 13.5 per cent would represent the sharpest correction in Irish economic activity since records began.

This dramatic slowdown in activity over such a short period of time came as quite a shock to the economic and political life of Ireland. The media continues to provide us with an almost daily diet of gloomy economic news, which has forced many people to stop reading newspapers and listening to news bulletins. The media obviously should not be criticised for reporting facts, but for many people it has become too much to bear. Indeed, in the summer of 2009 I broke my normal habit of holidaying in Ireland and went to the US for three weeks to try to get away from the justifiable doom and gloom that has enveloped the country.

The Government's Response

For any company or indeed economy, the quality of leadership is very important. If there is a belief that strong leadership is being provided, then workers in a company or citizens of a country will tend to react positively. Back in 1987 Ireland was in the midst of a very difficult economic and financial situation and confidence levels across society were pretty poor. At that stage Charles Haughey and Ray MacSharry in Government and Alan Dukes in opposition stood up and provided strong leadership. Regardless of whether one believed in their policy agenda or not, there was a strong sense that at last strong leadership was being provided and people bought into it. Domestic and international confidence in the country was given a major boost and the rest is history. During the crisis that commenced in 2008, there has been a general perception that such leadership was not being provided, and confidence levels remain poor, to put it mildly.

In July 2008, just after Brian Cowen took over as taoiseach and Brian Lenihan as minister for finance, the first measures were announced to address the deteriorating economic and financial climate. These measures included a deferral of the pending wage increases for ministerial and parliamentary office holders and other senior public servants, which had been recommended by the Review Body on Higher Remuneration in the Public Sector; a requirement for all departments, state agencies and local authorities (other than Health and Education) to cut their payroll bill by 3 per cent by the end of 2009; a reduction in the public relations and advertising spend by the state; and a cut in overseas development aid. It was estimated that these measures would deliver savings of €440 million in 2008 and €1 billion in 2009.

Given the rate at which the economy was deteriorating at that stage, these savings were pretty meaningless and were announced for cosmetic reasons rather than anything else. In other words, they were designed to convey the impression that the Government was recognising and addressing the emerging economic difficulties. The extent of the crisis demanded a much stronger response, but unfortunately it did not materialise. At that stage Brian Lenihan claimed that 'contrary to some of the commentary of recent weeks, our remarkable economic progress has not been reversed

20

overnight, and ... our economy continues to be strong and dynamic.'[12] It certainly did not feel like it at the time.

The measures announced in July 2008 did not convince anybody and by the end of the summer there was a growing sense that the country was rudderless. Confidence continued to plummet. The Government's political antennae cottoned on to this fact and again sought to do something about it.

The annual Budget is normally held in early December, but, following the Fianna Fáil party think-in in Galway in September 2008, it was decided to bring the Budget forward to October of that year. This decision perhaps reflected some belated recognition of the gravity of the evolving situation, but more likely it was a political strategy intended to deflect mounting criticism that the Government was well behind the curve in terms of recognising the gravity of the situation. Presumably, the Government believed that bringing the Budget forward to October would demonstrate a sense of urgency and control.

Whatever the motivation, at least an attempt was being made to address the mounting crisis and an air of expectation was built up that we were about to witness a 1987-style fiscal consolidation package. Alas, the Budget turned out to be a major anti-climax and disappointment, and one was left with the clear impression that either the Government did not recognise the gravity of the crisis, or, even if it did, it lacked the political will and clout to do anything about it.

The Budget contained a cocktail of small measures but there was nothing in it that inspired confidence that the evolving crisis was being addressed in a meaningful way.

The following were some of the key measures in the Budget:

- An additional 1 per cent levy was imposed on income up to €100,000 and 2 per cent on the balance over €100,000
- The standard rate of VAT was increased from 21 per cent to 21.5 per cent
- Deposit interest retention tax (DIRT) was increased to 23 per cent

- The maximum rate of stamp duty on non-residential property was reduced from 9 per cent to 6 per cent
- The capital gains tax rate was increased from 20 per cent to 22 per cent
- An air travel tax of €10 was introduced on longer journeys and €2 on shorter air journeys per person on all departures from Ireland
- Medical cards for people over 70 years of age were to become means tested; anyone not qualifying would receive a cash grant of €400, subject to means testing
- Automatic entitlement to Child Benefit would be reviewed
- Unreimbursed medical expenses would now only receive tax relief at the standard rate of tax
- Mortgage interest relief would be extended for first-time buyers but reduced for non-first-time buyers
- Employers who provide car parking for staff would have to pay a levy of €200
- A council levy of €200 per property would be introduced for non-principal private residences to cover rented accommodation and holiday homes
- Tax relief was introduced on bicycle purchases by those who decide to cycle to work.

The change to the medical card provision for the elderly was later amended following street protests by the grey population, while Brian Lenihan admitted at a Howth–Sutton–Baldoyle Chamber of Commerce lunch on 13 March 2009 that the decision to increase the VAT rate was a serious mistake that cost the state over €700 million in lost trade to Northern Ireland.[13] Although the VAT change was not significant in size, it coincided with a sharp temporary reduction in the UK tax rate and prompted thousands of Irish consumers to travel to Northern Ireland in 2008 and 2009 to fill their cars with alcohol, food and tobacco. When one admits to making a mistake, the normal expectation is that the mistake will be rectified at the first available opportunity. That did not happen.

It was hardly the type of budget needed in the face of the biggest economic and financial crisis facing the country in decades, but was deemed sufficient by the Government to bring order and stability to the public finances. Mr Lenihan described the Budget as 'a call to patriotic duty'.[14] On the night of the Budget I was so disillusioned and despondent that I retired to bed to watch *Desperate Housewives* rather than be subjected to any more media coverage of it.

By the end of 2008 it had become very clear that the economy was in a much more serious position than previously recognised by the Government. By the end of December the country had built up an Exchequer deficit of €12.7 billion, with tax revenues coming in over €8 billion behind target.[15] The previous July the Minister for Finance had said the shortfall would be €3 billion.[16]

In early February 2009 the people of Ireland were treated to the next instalment in the budgetary saga. This instalment was dominated by the introduction of a graduated pension-related deduction, which would apply to the total earnings of all public servants. The deduction was graduated so that lower income workers would pay a lower percentage of their earnings and higher paid workers a higher percentage. On average, the deduction would be 7.5 per cent of salary.

As predicted by many commentators, the budgetary saga did not end there. In April, the Minister for Finance was forced to introduce a Supplementary Budget to try to arrest the ongoing deterioration in the public finances. The key measures in this offering focused on a doubling of the income levies that had been introduced the previous October and a lower entry point, and a doubling of the various health levies. The main announcement in the Supplementary Budget was the setting up of the National Asset Management Agency (NAMA) under the aegis of the National Treasury Management Agency (NTMA) to purchase the development-related assets of the banks. It was proposed that NAMA would purchase the assets through the issue to the banks of government bonds. This would increase the gross national debt of the country, but it was envisaged that the assets taken in would offset some of it and that the cost of servicing the debt would be financed as much as possible from income accruing from the assets of the new agency. The liability to the state from this initiative will be significant, but the aim of Government is to clean bank balance sheets and get credit flowing again.

The changes announced in the April Supplementary Budget were intended to raise €3.3 billion in the final eight months of 2009 and €5 billion in a full year. Of the €3.3 billion to be raised in 2009, taxation increases were projected to raise €1.8 billion and the mainly vague spending cuts €1.5 billion.

Despite the stated aim of the Supplementary Budget to promote competitiveness and employment preservation, there was very little in it that could vaguely achieve either of these objectives. The Government again decided that the blunt instrument of increasing levies would be easier than addressing public spending in any meaningful way. Only time will tell if a policy of trying to tax an economy out of a deep recession will work, but the precedents are not particularly compelling. In July 2009, the *Report of the Special Group on Public Service Numbers and Expenditure Programmes,* outlining possible opportunities to cut government expenditure, was presented to the Minister for Finance. Presumably Budget 2010 in December 2009 will address some of the proposed cutbacks in expenditure.

Against this economic and budgetary background, it is not terribly surprising that the parties of Government were punished severely in the mid-2009 local and European elections. Ireland in the first half of 2009 found itself in the most difficult economic and financial situation since independence, and unfortunately domestic faith in the ability of the Government to lift the country out of the hole was not strong, nor does it appear to be improving.

Nobel Prize-winning economist Paul Krugman wrote a piece about Ireland in the *New York Times* in April 2009 headlined 'Erin go Broke'. In this piece, in a not very flattering way, he referred to Ireland as 'a cool snake-free version of coastal Florida'. He was writing in the context of Irish policy-makers allowing a monstrous property bubble to develop.

As is always the case with bubbles, when they burst the pain can be very severe. Considerable doubt surrounds the ability of NAMA to solve the banking crisis. The collapse of the economy, the banking system and the public finances is now costing the taxpayer dearly and will do so for years to come. However, Krugman was right – there's no getting away from the fact that the situation could have been so different if sane economic and financial policies had been pursued over the past decade.

2

The Irish Economy from the 1980s

Take a tiny, open ex-peasant economy. Place it next door to a much larger one, from which it broke away with great bitterness barely a lifetime ago. Infuse it with a passionate desire to enjoy the same lifestyle as its former masters, but without the same industrial heritage or natural resources. Inevitable result: extravagance, frustration, debt.

The Economist, 16 January 1988

The sudden and extreme collapse of the economy after 2008 has certainly come as a major shock to many in Ireland. This is particularly so for those of the current generation of workers who left school or college and who basically were in a position to get whatever job they wanted and earn practically whatever salary they wanted. For that generation it was very much a 'seller's market'. Back in the 1980s and early 1990s, when interviewing somebody for a job, one was faced with a candidate who was delighted to get an opportunity to attend an interview with the possibility of a job at the end of the process. By the end of the 1990s, this had changed and employers were left in little doubt as to how lucky they were to get the opportunity to interview somebody for a job. The power in the employer–worker relationship had certainly changed on the back of the Celtic Tiger. Some might describe this generation as arrogant, but in reality they were simply taking advantage of the opportunities and choices that were now available to them.

For that lucky generation, Celtic Tiger Ireland was a land of opportunity. You could be choosy about what job you would take, the purchase of a car or a house became a distinct possibility early in your working career, and of course lots of lavish lifestyle choices became available. Furthermore, if you got bored with your job, you could move on to a different and more lucrative job or decide to take a year out to go and travel the world. This was a very pleasing reality for the new Ireland, and it was inevitable that the younger generation would start to believe that this was what life was all about and that it represented a permanent reality. Unfortunately, this was never likely to be the case, and the reality is that such periods of opportunity, choice and prosperity represent the exception rather than the rule in Irish history.

Previous generations did not have much in the way of opportunity and were basically lucky to get a job, and, once they got it, the wisest thing to do was to hold on to it. After a relatively brief period of new-found prosperity and choice, the country is now reverting to kind. Jobs are being lost at a phenomenal pace, wages are being cut, and job insecurity and lack of choice are again becoming the norm. With the changed economic circumstances, the Celtic Tiger generation is in a state of shock and many are finding it quite difficult to adjust to the new reality.

They should not despair, however. The problems facing the economy today are not too dissimilar to the circumstances that prevailed in the 1980s. Through a combination of strong leadership, sound policy-making and no small amount of luck, Ireland pulled itself out of that crisis and created the platform for the Celtic Tiger. With strong leadership and sensible policy-making – both apparently lacking at the moment – it should be possible to get the economy back on a sustainable growth path again, but there should be no desire to create another Celtic Tiger. A more graceful and steady Celtic Cow would be a better symbol for what we should want in the future.

In light of Ireland's changed circumstances, it is worth reminding ourselves what the country was like in the 1980s. This chapter examines the set of circumstances that existed in the 1980s, and the policies that got us there, and, more importantly, outlines how we extricated ourselves from that particular mess. Although much has been written about this period in recent years, it is still worth revisiting to remind ourselves that where we are today as a nation is not without historical precedent, and that, no matter how great the crisis, there is always light at the end of the tunnel, provided the correct choices are made.

The Economist Provides a Wake-Up Call

For students of Irish economics in the first half of the 1980s the subject was a pretty depressing one and there was a tendency to wonder whether one was studying economics or fashion, such was the frequent use of terms like 'hair shirt' and 'belt tightening'. Ireland in those days was a very depressing place to inhabit because, despite considerable rhetoric from Government, the economy was a shambles. The public finances were in serious trouble, unemployment was dangerously high and there was a chronic balance of payments problem. Indeed, the overall health of the economy was in such disastrous shape that the IMF was allegedly showing an unhealthy interest in the country in 1986.

Early in 1988 *The Economist* ran a story on Ireland with a headline describing the country as the 'poorest of the rich'. I had just started working in the head office of Allied Irish Banks in an economic planning unit and was struck by the indignant reaction of the elite in that bank to this description of the country. Indeed, that reaction from senior bankers reflected the typical response from official Ireland, which ran along the lines of 'How dare the auld enemy cast such an aspersion on Ireland.' It was somewhat amusing to note that, as the housing bubble gathered momentum after 2005, the repeated warnings from the same UK magazine were rubbished by many and were regarded as the 'auld enemy' having another go at its former colony.

In Ireland, an attitude exists that, while it is bad enough to have domestic residents criticising the country, it is totally unacceptable to have anybody with the whiff of a British accent putting us down. I did not know enough at the time to comment on the veracity of *The Economist*'s assessment of the country. However, I sensed that – deep down – sensible, intelligent and thinking people actually realised back in 1988 that the magazine was spot on, but more importantly that something had to be done about it.

At that stage the country was arguably an economic and political failure, or an economic basket case to use a non-technical term. The GDP of the country was just 60 per cent of the European Community average, where it had been stuck for years, the unemployment rate exceeded 16 per cent of the labour force, the country was running massive balance of payments deficits and the public finance situation was one of the worst in the developed world. In 1985, the annual Exchequer deficit was equivalent to 12.3 per cent of GNP, the stock of outstanding national debt was equivalent to almost 118 per cent of GNP and interest on the national debt preempted almost one-third of total tax revenues.

Between 1980 and 1990 there was net outward emigration of 209,000 people from Ireland.[1] The typical profile of an emigrant was a young, highly educated individual with enough initiative to get up and leave the hopeless mess that was Ireland at the time. This brain drain robbed the country of many entrepreneurs and talented people. Consequently, the lack of any semblance of business or economic dynamism in the country during the 1980s should have come as no surprise.

In hindsight, the very negative and, some would claim, disparaging analysis by *The Economist* back in 1988 was exactly the kick in the backside that we required. It created a strong sense of indignation and failure. While many domestic commentators were providing similar analyses to that of *The Economist*, that a respected external vehicle pointed out the facts in such a stark way was particularly important. In my view, it made us realise just how bad things had become and that something would have to be done about it. Almost immediately, policy decisions began to be taken and implemented which laid the foundations for the Celtic Tiger.

The Fianna Fáil Election Manifesto of 1977

One needs to go back to the 1977 general election to get a clear understanding of the policy errors that resulted in the economic and fiscal crisis of the 1980s. The main opposition party at the time, Fianna Fáil, fought that general election on the basis of a populist manifesto that promised all things to all men. Unfortunately, the manifesto was successful in getting Fianna Fáil elected; thereafter, most of the populist policies promised in the manifesto were implemented and laid the foundations for the economic and fiscal crisis that was to come. It would be funny if it were not so serious to observe that much of the current crisis in the economy is also due to populist political policies that succeeded in getting successive governments elected, but which were ultimately not in the best long-term interests of the country. History just seems to keep repeating itself.

The infamous Fianna Fáil election manifesto of 1977 appears to fit very neatly under the banner of a dubious policy option and populist political decision-making. The background to that manifesto goes back to a meeting held in the home of Jack Lynch in June 1973 when a group called the Fianna Fáil Research and Support Services was formed to engage in more detailed policy analysis in order to provide better research services to the parliamentary party. This group produced a report[2] in September 1976 which set out the basis for the approach adopted in the later manifesto. The key message in that report was that the set of economic circumstances that prevailed at that time constituted 'the most serious economic challenge since the foundation of the state'. It went on to argue that, bad as the situation was, 'Fianna Fáil believe that rapid and decisive action can overcome these difficulties provided the correct policies are chosen and pursued single-mindedly and firmly.' This could have been written in 2009, the only difference being that Fianna Fáil was in opposition at that stage.

The manifesto itself makes for fascinating reading more than thirty years after its publication. In the introduction it is boldly stated that

> ...this manifesto gives young men and women their best chance to participate in the building of a better and stable future. It is a blueprint for leadership which, by the firm and just administration of law, esteem for enterprise, and concern for the individual, will bring back that sense of confidence and interdependence which is essential to the growth of peace and social progress, and of our cultural heritage and place among the nations of the world.[3]

One thing that is clear from this and from many other aspirational statements in the manifesto is that, despite the passage of more than thirty years, the language of politics and politicians has not changed very much. Grand visions are laid out, which are very rarely followed up with grand action plans.

The manifesto itself laid out an expansionary policy platform aimed at getting the economy out of the morass it was in at the time. A tax-cutting package of IR£160 million was planned, with the key elements centering around increasing income tax allowances for married couples, a reduction in the Social Welfare 'stamp' by IR£1 weekly for people earning less than IR£50 weekly, the abolition of annual road tax on all cars up to and including sixteen horse power, and the abolition of rates on all dwellings. Arguably, the latter decision created a mess for local government financing from which it has never fully recovered. It is ironic and interesting that speculation is currently rife concerning the introduction of some type of property tax on residential dwellings following the publication of the *Commission on Taxation Report* in September 2009.

The manifesto also had a strong spending element, which included IR£30 million to be spent on building and construction in order to create 5,000 jobs, IR£20 million to be spent on projects employing young people in order to create 5,000 jobs, and IR£50 million to be spent on extra Gardaí, teachers and other services. A campaign to 'buy Irish' was also promised in order to switch 3 pence in the pound from imports to home products. This is really uncanny, given the debate that is currently raging in Ireland about the change in sourcing of products that the global retail giant Tesco announced for the Irish market in May 2009 (see Chapter 8).

The manifesto also included other measures, such as the creation of a national understanding between employers and unions, which in many ways laid the foundations for the social partnership approach that was adopted in 1987.

The general stance adopted in the 1977 Fianna Fáil manifesto was basically an old-fashioned Keynesian fiscal stimulus approach, which is not terribly different from the policies now being pursued by President Obama in the US: cut taxes and increase spending in order to grow an economy out of a difficult situation.

In any event, the contents of the manifesto proved extremely popular with the electorate. Fianna Fáil, led by former Cork hurler Jack Lynch (prior to the days of hurling strikes in Cork), swept into government with a massive majority in the subsequent general election, and then set about implementing the Keynesian package. They implemented most of the measures promised, but history shows that the approach did not work and, by 1986, the economy and the public finances were in a much worse mess than in 1977; the country was effectively on the brink of bankruptcy.

In 1999, just after the Irish pound lost its legal status, I submitted an article to a now sadly defunct publication called the *Irish Banking Review*, which was published by the Irish Bankers' Federation. The article was an obituary for the Irish pound and traced its history from joining the European Exchange Rate Mechanism (ERM) in March 1979 until January 1999. In the first draft, I attributed the severe economic problems experienced in the mid-1980s to the flawed Fianna Fáil election manifesto of 1977. A few days later I received a call at work from the editor of the publication telling me that a meeting of the editorial board was taking place the following day, at which stage the various articles submitted would be assessed for publication. The sting in the tail became apparent when he also pointed out to me that a member of the editorial board was the chief architect of the 1977 manifesto and that I might expect a call from him.

I braced myself for a bruising phone call, and sure enough the following afternoon I received a call from Professor Martin O'Donoghue. It was anything but bruising. He very politely pointed out to me the error of my ways and attempted to put me straight. His main argument was that the elements of the manifesto were starting to work in 1978, but that events in 1979 conspired to blow it off track. The second oil crisis erupted in 1979 and later that year a change of leadership occurred in Fianna Fáil, when Charlie Haughey ousted Jack Lynch. Professor O'Donoghue argued to me that it was difficult to make a good assessment of the eventual outcome of the original programme once the disruption caused by the oil price shock and the change of leadership were taken into account.

One direct impact of the change of leadership in 1979 was that the efforts to control wages, in order to curb inflation, were effectively abandoned. The net result in the first half of the 1980s was strong growth in wages, high inflation, an ongoing spiral in current government expenditure, sharp cuts in capital spending and a very painful increase in the personal tax burden, which saw PAYE workers taking to the streets to protest in 1980. I took part in that protest, which would probably come as a bit of a surprise to the various trade unionists that I occasionally cross swords with today.

The Foundations of the Celtic Tiger

The Fianna Fáil manifesto of 1977 undoubtedly set the scene for the crisis situation that the economy found itself in by 1986. The national mood was very dark during that period and I remember Gay Byrne on the *Late Late Show* advising the young people of Ireland to emigrate to Australia because there was no hope for Ireland. It certainly felt that way at the time. The key issue for most people at that stage was that political leadership was awful and very few people had any faith in the ability of the political system to pull the economy out of the difficult situation. For those of us with similar feelings today, the ray of hope is that sometimes it is in moments of crisis that true leaders and sensible decisions emerge.

Back in the early 1990s, Kevin Gardiner, a UK-based economist who worked at the investment bank Morgan Stanley, coined the term 'Celtic Tiger' to describe the international phenomenon that Ireland was becoming at the time. He was basically comparing the Irish economy in the 1990s to the Asian miracle economies such as Taiwan and South Korea and decided on the catchy title 'Celtic Tiger' to describe what he saw as a rapidly emerging economy. The term has become firmly enshrined in Irish popular vocabulary and has been used and abused with frightening alacrity over the years. In fact, it had reached the stage by 2000 when the very mention of the term started to elicit feelings of nausea within me and I came around to the view that the inventor of the term should be 'boiled in his own spittle'. In some ways it is almost a relief today that the Celtic Tiger has expired as an entity. Unfortunately, mostly out of convenience, the term remains part of the popular lexicon. It recurs frequently in this book, for example.

The Celtic Tiger period should really be described as the years between 1994 and 2000. During that period GDP growth averaged just over 9 per cent per annum, with exports making the most important contribution to growth. Over this period, the annual average growth in the volume of exports was a staggering 18 per cent. GNP per head of population increased by over 70 per cent. To put this latter statistic in context, this metric had increased by just 28 per cent in the fourteen-year period up to 1994.[4] This was truly impressive stuff.

During the Celtic Tiger years there were many cynics and critics who refused to admit that the economy was doing well and even today we hear people complain that the Celtic Tiger passed them by or failed to growl for them. At a macro level, such doubts and reservations are easily dispelled by the facts. Between 1960 and 1985, income per head of population in Ireland remained pretty stable relative to the Organisation for Economic Cooperation and Development (OECD) average and was in fact surpassed by a number of nations that we would now regard with some economic disdain. However, by the time the phenomenon ended, income per head of population had moved well ahead of the EU and OECD average, where it still remains today despite the collapse in incomes in 2008 and 2009. Furthermore, the unemployment rate fell from 15.7 per cent of the labour force in 1993 to just 4.3 per cent by the first quarter of 2000 and the number of people in employment increased from 1.2 million to 1.7 million over the same period.[5]

It is important to point out at the outset that the transformation was not the result of a lucky accident or any single policy initiative, but rather was due to a combination of factors, some fortuitous and some deliberate. All of these factors coincided to push the economy on to a higher growth platform. It is also important to point out that the country was coming from a very low base. Poor policy-making and populist politics had contrived to prevent the economy from emerging for a couple of decades at least.

Much has been written since 1987 about the causes of this dramatic economic renaissance and, as is the case with most economic issues, it has proved very difficult to achieve a solid consensus on its origins. However, without going into an academic treatise on the causes, it is possible to identify a number of key factors, all of which contributed to varying degrees.

Fiscal Policy of Government

Faced with economic and financial crisis in 1987, the new Government got its act together in a significant way. During the general election campaign of February 1987, Charles

Haughey, the leader of the Fianna Fáil party in opposition, vigorously attacked the public expenditure cuts proposed by Fine Gael in government, but, once in power, he did an amazing about-turn and, along with Minister for Finance Ray MacSharry, proceeded to cut public expenditure in a relatively dramatic fashion. Such measures were met with only muted popular opposition because most sensible people realised that the mess had to be addressed or the IMF would come in to run what was in effect a country on the brink of bankruptcy. Never before was a finance minister able to carry out such draconian measures with such ease and with relatively little opposition – apart from a few noisy marches. Any opposition was promptly swept aside by MacSharry, who quickly earned the nickname 'Mac the Knife'. Fine Gael's efforts in government between 1983 and 1987 to rectify the fiscal situation, however unsuccessful, at least provided MacSharry with a model of sorts.

The process of putting the nation's finances in order was also hugely facilitated by the 'Tallaght Strategy', adopted in 1987 by the leader of the opposition Alan Dukes. He agreed to provide constructive opposition as long as the Government pursued sound fiscal policies. This strategy was a brave one for Dukes and in a fair world he would have become a folk hero. However, no one ever claimed that it is a fair world, and Mr Dukes's bravery and vision were rewarded with his removal as leader of Fine Gael in 1990 following a difficult presidential election for his party, and indeed he lost his Dáil seat in the 2002 general election. Thankfully, history has been kind to Dukes and his crucial role back in 1987 is now generally acknowledged by fair-minded people; he has become a leading voice of sense and reason in the Irish commentariat.

On the back of MacSharry's fiscal consolidation programme, the Exchequer borrowing requirement fell from 11.4 per cent of GNP in 1986 to a surplus equivalent of 3.6 per cent of GNP by 2000.[6] This improvement in the fiscal situation facilitated a steady easing of the personal tax burden, a move that encouraged effort, initiative and much higher labour force participation. There has been considerable academic debate about the real impact of the fiscal measures in 1987. Dermot McAleese of Trinity College Dublin posits the notion of 'expansionary fiscal contraction',[7] which describes a phenomenon that appears to fly in the face of economic logic. Intuitively it may not appear obvious how a sharp tightening of fiscal policy would have a positive impact on economic growth. The argument used by McAleese to justify his theory is that a reduction in the budget deficit would create the expectation of a lower tax burden in the future and this wealth effect would act as a spur to private sector demand. Furthermore, the associated reduction in interest rates, as international investor confidence in the economy improved, would support the recovery in economic activity. This is exactly what appears to have happened.

Persistently high interest rates had been a serious problem for the economy for some years. Back in March 1979, when I was studying Leaving Cert economics, the Irish pound became a member of the Exchange Rate Mechanism (ERM) of the European Monetary System (EMS), which was a semi-fixed exchange rate regime based upon member counties maintaining a tight trading relationship with the German Deutsche Mark. The theory was that, by locking into a strong currency like the Deutsche Mark, Ireland would achieve trust from international investors and would eventually attain German-style interest rates and inflation as capital flowed into the country. The theory was sound, but the practical application of it was not so good. We did not behave as a country in a fixed exchange rate regime should – wages and public spending were not controlled and the result was that international confidence in the Irish pound did not improve and we ended up with much higher interest rates than Germany. Our experience in the European Economic and Monetary Union (EMU), which will be discussed in Chapter 6, suggests, again, that history has a tendency to repeat itself in this country. As mentioned in Chapter 1, in the middle of 2009 we had to pay 2 per cent more interest than Germany to borrow money for ten years, despite the fact that the country is part of a monetary union with Germany. This differential reflected the fact that international borrowers believed that Ireland had become a high-risk country to lend money to, hence they demanded a premium to take this risk. This is exactly the situation that prevailed in the 1980s. Back in 1987, when economic policy-making became consistent with the exchange rate obligation, international confidence improved very quickly and interest rates started to fall sharply, giving a major boost to economic activity.

Foreign Direct Investment

Ireland was an economically depressed place back in the 1950s, after years of the closed and introverted economic policies pursued by Eamon De Valera. Thankfully, in the late 1950s, as the De Valera influence was being expunged from memory, policy-makers led by Seán Lemass realised that, as a very small economy with a limited domestic market, economic policy would have to change. A key part of this change was the recognition that the country would have to be opened up to trade and investment, and that getting foreign companies to invest in the country could pay huge dividends. Policies were put in place to try to attract such companies into the country, including favourable corporation tax rates and generous grants. This policy was sound and Ireland in subsequent decades achieved considerable success in attracting foreign direct investment, particularly from the US, in industries such as financial services, information technology, and chemicals and pharmaceuticals. The success in attracting foreign direct investment from the US was primarily due to the low corporation tax rate regime, the availability of a young, highly educated and English-speaking labour force, and Ireland's geographical market position within the EU. In the period from 1997 to 2002, the volume of merchandise exports out of Ireland recorded annual average growth rates of 15.1 per cent.[8]

As well as putting sensible policies in place, we were was also lucky, in the sense that US companies were becoming very expansionary on the back of a corporate earnings boom in the 1990s and they wanted to gain a foothold in the emerging single European market. Ireland proved to be a good host, quite simply because the general environment was conducive to profit maximisation. Some people claim that US companies have an affinity to the country for cultural reasons, but the fact is that the US corporate model has no time for sentimentality and the sole determinant of investment decisions is profit. For many years Ireland satisfied that criterion, but obviously the model is now under serious pressure and we will have to change if it is to continue to play in the foreign direct investment space.

From a regional economic point of view, the foreign direct investment experience was positive. The arrival of a major US multinational corporation gave life to ailing towns and cities around the country, and spawned many secondary jobs. The downside of this of course is that the closure or downscaling of a major multinational employer in a region can create serious economic and social difficulties for that region. The trick is to try to ensure that the environment is such that downscaling is not considered in the first place. That is a very difficult challenge.

The arrival of foreign direct investment also had a beneficial impact on work practices. Basically, the Irish working environment had to change in order to accommodate more modern industries. The foreign direct investment boom propelled the country into the twentieth century and is now dragging us into the twenty-first century.

Social Partnership

Different people have different views on the contribution of the social partnership process to the recovery story. The model commenced in 1988 and originally consisted of employers, farmers, workers and Government coming together to agree on wage rates in return for commitments on taxation. Trade unions agreed to accept lower wage settlements in return for an easing of the personal tax burden. As the process evolved over the following 20 years, various other bodies got involved and it evolved into a process that determined a broader range of social and economic policies.

In its early days, social partnership certainly brought greater stability and certainty for employers in regard to wages following decades of irresponsible trade union behavior and widespread industrial unrest, which seriously damaged the competitiveness and reputation of the economy. However, I believe that it passed its sell-by date and had outlived its usefulness by the late 1990s, once the economy reached effective full employment. It then became part of the problem rather than part of the solution. An assessment of social partnership is in Chapter 6, but suffice to say at this stage that I have not been a fan of the process for the past decade.

Membership of the European Union

Since Ireland joined the Common Market in 1973, it has been a very enthusiastic member of the European family, notwithstanding a few European treaty blips, the most recent of which was the rejection of the Lisbon Treaty in 2008. This was subsequently reversed in a second referendum in October 2009. Much of our enthusiasm for the EU was driven by a desire, both political and economic, to reduce the historical dependence on the UK. In the past Ireland was totally dependent on the UK and sterling from an economic perspective, and the Irish economy unfortunately inherited many of the ills resulting from the abject failure of the UK authorities to manage its economy in the 1960s and 1970s. It was a case of when the UK caught a cold, Ireland got the flu. There was also, of course, the political imperative driven by 800 years of history. Many of us believed that anything which reduced our dependence on the UK was by definition good, and anything that increased that dependence was by definition bad. A senior civil servant told me in the early 1990s that policy-making had at its core a desire to reduce the economic and political dependence on the UK.

Membership of the EU and the deepening of that membership fundamentally changed the nature of the Irish economy, both in terms of allowing trade to diversify away from the previously dominant UK market and the funding received from the EU to improve the structures of the economy. At their peak in 1991, net receipts from the EU were equivalent to 6.2 per cent of GDP. Some UK commentators have claimed in the past that Ireland's economic success was due to the largesse of the European taxpayer, but the reality is that, while EU funding reinforced a number of other positive factors, it was not the only factor that influenced our success. Admittedly, the funding did come at an opportune time, when many other factors were falling into place.

As part of its commitment to all things European, Ireland embraced the notion of the EMU enthusiastically in the early 1990s. All policy-making became focused on ensuring that Ireland would satisfy the Maastricht convergence criteria and would become a founding member of the EMU and the single European currency in January 1999. These criteria related to variables such as inflation, long-term interest rates, the Government's annual borrowing requirement and the outstanding level of government debt. Ireland performed very impressively during the 1990s and easily qualified for membership, unlike some of our more illustrious European neighbours such as France and Italy, who had to fudge the criteria to qualify. Ireland qualified on its own merits and became a founding member of the single European currency in 1999.

The single currency delivered a certain level of exchange rate stability, but was limited by the UK's non-participation in the European dream. More importantly, membership of the single currency delivered a historically low level of interest rates, which gave a significant boost to economic activity. In 1990, for example, the three-month interbank interest rate stood at 11.5 per cent, but by the end of 1999 this had fallen to just 3.3 per cent. This acted as a major boon to Irish business and consumers, and helped generate a borrowing binge the results of which we are now trying to come to terms with.

Exchange Rate

Manipulation of the Irish exchange rate also played an important role in the export boom experienced in Ireland. In 1993 the Irish pound was devalued by 10 per cent after a period of protracted pressure on its position within the ERM following sterling's exit from the ERM on 'Black Wednesday' in September 1992. In the period between sterling's exit from the ERM and the eventual devaluation of the Irish pound more than four months later, there was a concerted effort by the then Minister for Finance Bertie Ahern to fend off the inevitable. Interest rates were raised to 100 per cent to defend the Irish currency and anybody who dared suggest that devaluation was inevitable, or even that it might be a good idea, was subjected to the ire of official Ireland.

A 'black list' was drawn up of those who favoured devaluation and official complaints were made to employers of those people. I worked in Bank of Ireland at the time and was the subject of such a complaint by the Department of Finance following a note I sent out to a major corporate client in November 1992 advising that a devaluation of between 8 and 10 per cent was inevitable. This note found its way into the hands of a major competitor of Bank of Ireland, who in turn passed it on to the economics correspondent at RTÉ, who mentioned it in a news broadcast. It subsequently made its way to the Department of Finance. A complaint was made and I had my wrist slapped.*

In any event, a devaluation of 10 per cent occurred at the end of January 1993. Far from this resulting in serious reputational damage to the economy and the financial system, as had been warned by many 'Irish patriots', the devaluation was a resounding success. It gave a serious boost to the competitiveness of the exporting sector and provided the platform for the very impressive export performance that

---

*Somewhat strangely, history repeated itself in the early months of 2009 due to comments made by me in an interview with the *Financial Times*

was delivered during the Celtic Tiger years. Growth took off immediately and continued until very recently.

Demographics, Labour Supply and Productivity

The potential growth rate of an economy is the level of economic activity that an economy can expect to achieve if all economic resources are fully utilised. Growth in employment and productivity gives us potential growth. In the second half of the 1990s, growth in employment averaged 5.5 per cent per annum and growth in productivity was estimated at around 3 per cent in real terms.[9] In an Irish context, productivity is difficult to measure because of the transfer pricing activities of multinationals. However, a conservative estimate of 3 per cent would suggest that the potential growth rate of the economy in the second half of the 1990s was around 8.5 per cent. Economies, of course, do not necessarily always realise their potential, but Ireland did due to a combination of good luck and sound economic policies.

The potential growth rate of the Irish economy in the 1990s was driven higher by solid productivity growth and strong inflows to the labour market. Demographics played an important role in this. Ireland's historically Catholic ethos had created a situation where the number of births in Ireland grew strongly during the 1970s and peaked at 74,000 in 1980. This 'baby boom' resulted in strong growth in the young labour force in the 1990s and added significantly to the supply side potential of the economy during that decade. Due to the introduction of free second-level education in 1967 and subsequent strong investment in all levels of education, the quality of that labour force growth was good. The abundant supply of skilled young labour proved very attrac-

---

concerning the risks involved in Ireland's deteriorating public finances, which resulted in another formal complaint from the Department of Finance. After more than 20 years commentating on the Irish economy; it strikes me that it is more important to say the right thing rather than be right in what you say. This is sad and worrying because, without proper open debate, problems will never be solved.

tive to companies in the US and Europe who faced labour shortages in their own markets.

The bottom line is that the economy was a direct beneficiary of the old Catholic value which held that sex should be used exclusively for procreation and which shunned any type of birth control. Birth rates have subsequently slowed and one can only wonder if Barry Desmond, who was Minister for Health in the 1970s, will go down in history as a contributing factor to the demise of the Irish economic renaissance, now that more liberal values have permeated the national psyche and resulted in a sharp drop in birth rate and family size over the past decade.

The flows into the labour force were also driven by the decline in unemployment, higher labour force participation rates for both males and females, and steady inward migration. The unemployment rate declined from 15 per cent of the labour force in 1989 to 4.3 per cent in 2000.[10] Over the same period, total employment in the economy expanded from 1.11 million people to 1.67 million.[11] Between 1990 and 1995 there was net outward migration of 24,000, but between 1996 and 2000 there was net inward migration of 87,000.[12] These factors boosted the labour supply and pushed up the potential growth rate of the economy.

The Post-Celtic Tiger Years

It is important to recognise that the 1990s should be seen as a catch-up period for the Irish economy. In that decade, Ireland effectively moved from being a seriously underdeveloped economy to being a more modern, developed one. The sort of growth rates that Ireland enjoyed typically characterise a catching-up process of this nature, but the important point is that, once the catch-up phase is complete, economic growth inevitably tends to slow of its own volition as resources such as labour start to become scarcer.

The expectation coming into the new millennium was that growth in the labour force would ease due to the fact that the economy was operating at virtually full employment and the army of the unemployed was depleted. While there was some slowdown in Irish growth between 2001 and 2007, annual growth in GDP still averaged an impressive 5.6 per cent.[13] The growth potential of the economy was given a significant boost by strong inward migration, particularly after the first wave of EU accession when Ireland, unlike most of our EU partners, decided to open up its borders to immigrants from those accession countries. Between 2001 and 2007, there was net inward migration of 357,000 people, which gave a significant boost to labour force growth and hence to the growth potential of the economy.

Although growth in the economy eased modestly after 2000, the nature of economic growth did change significantly after 2001, with exports making a significantly lesser contribution to growth. Consumer spending and house building became the big drivers of economic activity after 2001. Between 2001 and 2007 annual average growth in exports slowed to 5.8 per cent, compared to growth of 17.7 per cent between 1994 and 2000. In the period 2001 to 2007, consumer spending recorded annual average growth of 5 per cent. Over the same period, 508,473 new houses were completed compared to 211,240 new houses over the previous five years.

Table 1 demonstrates clearly the changing nature of the Irish economy. It breaks down the sectoral employment situation in 2007 compared to 1998. The key trend evident is the decline in employment in agriculture, forestry and fishing, and industrial production. Construction, health, and financial and business services recorded strong growth. These changing trends in employment paint a clear picture of how the economy has evolved over the past decade, but also pose some serious questions about the quality of growth in the Irish labour market. Productive sectors are in decline, while many of the sectors growing in significance are not sustainable in the longer term. Indeed, they have not even been sustained into 2008 and 2009.

Chapters 3 to 6 will examine in more detail the evolution of the economy in the 'noughties' and how the seeds were sown for the deep recession that commenced in 2008.

Table 1: Employment by Sector

Sector	1998 %	2007 %
Agriculture, Forestry & Fishing	**9.1**	**5.4**
Production Industries	**20.2**	**14.0**
Construction	**8.4**	**13.4**
Wholesale & Retail	14.1	14.0
Hotels & Restaurants	6.5	6.3
Transport, Storage & Communication	5.8	5.8
Financial & Business Services	11.4	13.6
Public Administration & Defence	4.7	4.8
Education	6.2	6.6
Health	7.7	10.1
Other Services	5.8	6.0

Source: CSO, *Quarterly National Household Survey.*

However, all is not lost. We must learn lessons from the 1980s and from the mistakes made in the late 1990s and into the 2000s. The set of circumstances that gave rise to the Celtic Tiger are not likely to occur in such a combination again, so we must ensure that a more sustainable economic model is now re-created. Just as was the case in 1987, strong, visionary political leadership will be required to get the economy back on track. It is incumbent on the body politic to deliver such leadership and vision.

3

The Sacrifice of Quality

The gross national product of a country does not allow for the health of our children, the quality of their education or the joy of their play. It does not include the beauty of our poetry or the strength of our marriages, the intelligence of our public debate or the integrity of our public officials. It measures neither our wit nor our courage, neither our wisdom nor our learning, neither our compassion nor our devotion to our country. It measures everything in short, except that which makes life worthwhile.

Robert Kennedy, 18 March 1968

The Quality and Sustainability of Ireland's Economic Growth

Ireland has undoubtedly come through a period of remarkable and unprecedented economic growth. Lots of wealth was generated over the past fifteen years or so, many jobs were created, exciting opportunities were opened up to the citizens of the country. An air of gloom was very definitely replaced by a greater sense of hope and optimism than had been seen since the 1960s. On most economic metrics Ireland has been doing very well up until recently, and it is not terribly surprising that our policy-makers and politicians have been more than happy to take the plaudits.

While welcoming much of the change that has occurred in Ireland, I have generally been somewhat on the sceptical side of the fence in more recent years and I have tried to reflect this in my contributions to various media, but particularly in my weekly column in the *Irish Examiner*. Indeed, during my days in Bank of Ireland, when I was not generally encouraged to speak my mind, I wrote a weekly column in *Business and Finance* magazine under a pseudonym where I also gave vent to my feelings on the manner in which the Irish economy and Irish society were developing. I am not arrogant enough to suggest that I got it all right over the years, indeed far from it, but I have been concerned for some years that the whole focus of policy-making was on maximising economic growth and job creation, without much consideration being given to the quality, or indeed the sustainability, of that growth. If my epitaph is ever written, I hope that it would focus on my preoccupation with quality rather than quantity.

Economic growth per se is great, but it is not the 'be all and the end all', nor should it be. At the end of the day, economic growth is only as good as the positive fruits that flow from it that impact directly on the quality of life of the nation. It is also important to consider the sustainability of growth. It is much better to move gradually towards one's target, rather than making a mad dash and running out of steam before the destination is reached. In my view, Ireland made a mad dash for growth and we now know that much of the growth was of dubious quality and was not sustainable. For that, our policy-makers and in my view Bertie Ahern, our political leader for most of the period, must bear most if not all of the responsibility.

I certainly believe that the Irish economy and Irish society are now facing immense challenges and there is a serious lack of faith in the ability and willingness of the political and state system to meet these challenges. I will address these problems and challenges later in the book. In this chapter and Chapters 4 to 6, I will examine what I would regard as some of the key policy errors in recent years that contributed to the current difficulties that we are facing as an economy and as a society, and that have given rise to the justifiable sense of disillusionment and lack of faith. However, there is not a lot to be gained from engaging in a blame game, but there is a lot to be gained from analysing and understanding the mistakes that were made and, more importantly, to ensure that they are not repeated.

The key failing of Bertie Ahern and his policy-makers over the past decade, in my view, was their inability to differentiate between the quantity of activity being generated and the quality and sustainability of that activity. Basically, we pumped valuable and scarce resources into sectors of the economy that were never going to be sustainable in the longer term, and we focused way too much attention on the amount of money spent on public services, without taking due account of the output from that spending. If there is one lesson to be learned for the future from Ireland's performance over the past decade, it is that we should put quality absolutely ahead of quantity in future economic and financial planning.

Until recently, a perusal of many of Ireland's economic and financial indicators, from economic growth, to employment, to government spending, to the state of the public finances, does indeed suggest that we Irish have never had it so good. However, on deeper examination, it does become apparent that the Government built up way too much dependence on sectors that were never going to be sustainable in the longer term; and though we generated and spent a lot of money as a country, one does wonder if, with better leadership and policy-making, the money could have been spent in a better manner.

Measuring Economic Success

The Central Intelligence Agency (CIA) is a repository of useful economic and political information and intelligence, although some might tend to question its objectivity. When I see some investment group or other promoting the latest property investment hotspot, the first thing I tend to do is go to the CIA website (www.cia.gov) to check it out, and I normally get a pretty good objective picture that I can use to warn off the poor suckers who might be tempted to plough their hard-earned money, or, worse still, the hard-earned money of some bank, into some place like Cape Verde. Its 'World Fact Book' provides very good comparative economic data which allows the user to make comparisons between economic variables in up to 266 world entities. For economic and political nerds, this is nirvana.

As we wallow in gloom here in Ireland in the face of an unprecedented economic and financial shock, and as we convince ourselves that we are totally doomed, it is interesting to note that, according to the CIA, Ireland ranks eleventh out of 229 countries in terms of 'GDP per capita'. The CIA is telling us that if we divide up the total Irish economic cake between the 4.2 million people living in the country, each person would get a piece of cake that would be the eleventh biggest of 229 countries considered, and the second biggest piece of cake received by an individual in the EU.

It is also interesting to note that Ireland does score pretty well in the Human Development Index compiled by the United Nations (UN).[1] This index is based on a belief that, while economic growth is a useful indicator of development, it is limited in its ability to capture how expanding income translates into human development. The index attempts to combine data on incomes, education and health into a single index to give a deeper understanding of how countries are doing. In 2006, Ireland was ranked fifth out of 179 countries around the world.

Despite these findings, it is still interesting to delve deeper into how the Irish economy and Irish society have been doing in recent years.

Economists and politicians love using statistics to prove whatever point they want to make. For a politician in government, the GDP per capita metric for Ireland is an indicator that one could dwell on for a long time. The fact that each Irish person on average gets to eat the second largest piece of cake in the EU is impressive. However, just like any other piece of economic data, how it is interpreted is very important.

While GDP is a useful measure of economic activity, it is crude and does not tell the whole story. For example, it does not tell us very much about issues such as the quality of education, the quality of health services, commuting times to work, traffic congestion, life expectancy, quality of water, quality of food, crime levels, pollution, voluntary activities, or, most importantly of all, how the GDP is distributed amongst the population. GDP in absolute terms or in per capita terms basically tells us what the size of the cake is, but tells us very little about the ingredients used to make the cake, how it is baked, to whom it is given, or, most importantly, what it tastes like.

There is also the issue of the black or shadow economy. These terms describe the part of the economy that is outside the realm of officialdom or, in other words, those economic activities that do not appear on the radar of the Revenue Commissioners or other official agencies. Such activities would include 'nixers' – work that is not registered for tax purposes – and illegal smuggling. The illicit drugs trade is clearly a major growth area in most if not all economies, but it is not captured by official statistics. It is estimated that, back in 2002, the black economy in Ireland was equivalent to 16 per cent of GDP, which is almost €21 billion. At the best of times, one can only guess the size of the black economy because, by definition, no statistics are available. However, we can take it that it is a significant size. And in an environment of recession and rising taxes, which is where Ireland finds itself in 2009, one would normally expect the size of the black economy to increase.

In Ireland's case there is one other major caveat that must be considered when talking about variables such as GDP per capita. That caveat is called net factor income from the rest of the world (NFI). This figure would primarily include the difference between the profits and dividends that are paid back to Ireland by Irish companies operating overseas, and those paid abroad by foreign-owned companies operating in Ireland. It also includes the interest paid on the foreign component of Ireland's national debt and also the interest paid to any Irish holders of foreign government debt. Given Ireland's dependence on foreign multinationals, the NFI figure is significant because companies like Pfizer and Intel repatriate significant amounts of money back to their home countries. In 2008, the net outflow of monies from Ireland totalled a significant sum of just over €27 billion. When this figure is taken away from GDP, which totalled almost €182 billion, we are left with a GNP of almost €155 billion.[2] Given that this net financial outflow of €27 billion does not find its way into Irish pockets, it should not really be included as part of real Irish income. On the basis of GNP per capita, Ireland does not look quite as appealing, but the country has still done pretty well.

The most commonly used international standard is GDP, so on the international stage most economic metrics are discussed relative to GDP. However, it is more appropriate to consider the smaller GNP number in the Irish context when measuring such things as the health or education spend as a percentage of national income. However, both GNP and GDP do not capture the quality of life.

Despite these reservations about GDP, the fact is that it is still important because countries with a high GDP tend, in general, to perform better under headings like life expectancy, educational attainment and general quality of life. There are, of course, always going to be exceptions to everything, but the general rule tends to hold true.

The concept of economic welfare tries to take the notion of economic growth a step further to examine how happy people are and what their quality of life is like. However, people's sense of well-being is obviously very subjective: if you ask people how happy they are it can vary from day to day, or indeed from one time of day to another. As I write this, the Waterford hurling team has just lost the Munster Final, so I am not in a particularly happy frame of mind. It is also, of course, the nature of particular people to adopt the poor mouth and never admit they are feeling content with life, even if they are.

Anecdotally, from listening to radio, reading newspapers and magazines and generally observing people's behaviour, one does get the sense of a disillusionment in society at the moment. Many people believe that, after a decade and a half of the strongest economic growth in history, we are still left with a bevy of serious problems in the economy and society in general. People are not happy with a health service that appears to be inferior to those of our international peers, with continued long waiting lists and patients being confined to hospital trolleys for long periods of time. In the education system, class size is still very large; the ability to cater, for example, for children for whom English is not the first language or children with special needs is seriously limited; the provision of basic IT services is problematic in many schools; and the quality of a number of school buildings is not what one would expect in a first-world developed economy. People are also unhappy with house prices and the cost of living, and are growing increasingly concerned about the level of serious and petty crime in Irish society.

The levels of alcohol and drug abuse are also reaching frightening proportions and this is becoming a serious concern for most parents. Alcohol in particular has become an epidemic that is seriously undermining the social fabric of Irish life. Alcohol abuse is nothing new in Ireland, but, as our incomes soared during the Celtic Tiger years, we could afford to buy a lot more, and that we did. Alcohol occupies a very important place in Irish society and a frightening drink culture is perpetuated by the adult population; the younger population is taking up the alcohol baton with enthusiasm. Alcohol consumption in Ireland is as acceptable as food consumption and it dominates all of the key stages of our life cycle – when our childern are born we wet their heads, when they get married we celebrate with alcohol, and when they die we drink them into the grave. This is obviously not unique to Ireland, but we are well up there in terms of alcohol abuse.

This is just a snapshot of how many Irish now perceive Ireland. A common concern is that, if we failed to address these problems and shortcomings during the prosperous period of the Celtic Tiger, what hope will we have in more straitened economic times that look likely to last for a considerable period?

Some would of course argue that we have never had it so good and that negative perceptions are simply wrong. It is generally politicians of the government variety who tend to make such arguments. The truth is that, whether it is the reality or not, perception tends to become the reality.

How Good Was It?

Up to 2007 we became very accustomed to government politicians pointing out to all and sundry how much economic growth and employment was being created in the economy. However, they never stood back, at least not in public, and questioned the quality and sustainability of the economic growth and employment that was being created.

It should have struck them as a bit strange, and perhaps somewhat worrying, that in the five-year period to 2007 more than 57 per cent of the jobs created in the economy were in construction and the public sector. These trends were never likely to be sustainable because inevitably the point had to come when enough concrete had been pumped into the ground and enough houses had been built. We certainly reached that point in 2008. Likewise, there is a financial limit to how many jobs can be created in the public sector. After all, public sector employment has to be paid for out of either taxation or borrowing. The EU in theory places a limit on how much the country can borrow under the terms of the Stability and Growth Pact. On top of this, in Budget after Budget, both Charlie McCreevy and Brian Cowen as finance ministers stood up in the Dáil boasting about how many thousand more workers were being removed from the tax net, while at the same time the Exchequer coffers were becoming more and more dependent on the construction sector. This had the effect of narrowing the tax base consistently over a number of years and in 2008 the tax take started to collapse as the construction boom ended with a bang. This situation should have, in theory, put a cap on employment in the public sector, but it did not.

So we have now arrived at a point where the two biggest drivers of employment in the economy have gone into retreat, and it is hard to see where the fresh job creation is going to come from. In addition, much of the employment created in the financial and business services sectors had been driven strongly by the housing and mortgage boom, and so the prospects of future employment creation in these sectors do not look too healthy either.

There is also a huge question mark over the other driver of economic growth and employment – the consumer. The heavily indebted Irish consumer is now under serious pressure from wage cuts, tax increases and rising unemployment. This is now starting to affect employment in the wholesale and retail sectors, with retailers shutting up shop on a weekly basis.

Another aspect of Ireland's recent employment performance was the extent to which non-Irish nationals fuelled the economic boom. In the first quarter of 2008, 342,700 non-Irish nationals accounted for 19.2 per cent of total employment in the economy. Of these, 43,200 worked in the construction industry, with 30,300 of these from the EU accession states. This number of non-nationals working in construction had fallen to just 19,100 by the second quarter of 2009 and is still falling.[3] There was certainly a sense in recent years that Ireland was bringing in workers from overseas to fuel the housing boom, or in other words they were basically coming in to build houses for themselves, but that situation was never likely to be sustainable and is now unravelling at an alarming pace.

Irish policy-makers became totally intoxicated by the riches that were being generated by the construction boom and allowed the banking sector to become exposed to a dramatic property bubble. Due to planning failures and a policy of facilitating rampant growth in house prices, thousands of workers were forced to buy homes up to 50 miles or more outside of Dublin and to commute on sub-standard public transport to Dublin to work. One morning I had stopped on my bicycle at traffic lights on Dublin's Baggot Street at 6.30 a.m. and noticed a car pulling up beside me with a young baby asleep in the back seat, obviously waiting to be dropped off at a crèche. It struck me that morning that the quality of life forced on many people due to serious policy failures was not very desirable, to put it mildly. Indeed, the social implications of a generation reared in crèches and minded at weekends by stressed-out and heavily indebted parents remains to be seen.

Another reason for the new crèche culture, and an example of how the Government didn't prioritise quality of life in their policy-making, was Minister for Finance Charlie McCreevy's decision to introduce individualisation of the tax system in Budget 2000. Prior to this move, the single person's tax band was doubled for married couples, but following the change each individual has his or her own standard rate band. The tax band for two-income married couples would be set at double the individual band, but not for a one-income married couple. This caused a considerable deterioration in the relative tax position of the one-income married couple and was basically an attempt to use a financial 'stick' to force stay-at-home spouses back into the paid workforce, thereby increasing labour force participation rates. The problem was that, while more and more people, particularly women, came back into the paid workforce, an adequate child-care support system was not put in place. On the evening this policy was announced, RTÉ's economics correspondent George Lee was very upset by the proposal and his emotional coverage of the issue elicited a complaint to RTÉ from Government. Perhaps this reflected his own personal situation, but more probably it indicated his anger at a socially regressive change in the tax code.

On the evening after that Budget, I was doing a briefing hosted by Bank of Ireland in Cork. In the middle of my presentation a mobile phone rang loudly in the audience, which elicited from me the wish that it was my wife letting me know she was going back to paid employment. Alas, it was not and I am still at a relative disadvantage due to this initiative that was further developed in subsequent budgets.

The policy of individualisation made sense from an economic perspective as it would increase labour force participation in an economy where, at the time, labour shortages were prevalent. However, from a social perspective, individualisation was draconian and forced more and more children into an inadequate child-care system.

Policy-makers also allowed the cost of doing business to spiral upwards and the competitiveness of the economy to be seriously undermined (see Chapter 5). The public finances became unbalanced and unsustainable. Public spending was allowed to grow, with value for taxpayers' money apparently not featuring very strongly in the thought process. This is explored in more detail in Chapter 6.

During the period under consideration, the Irish economy and its financial system became too reliant on the property and construction sectors. This practice was proved to be unsustainable from 2007 onwards, and the bursting of the housing bubble had an impact on the overall economy and the financial system that has proved to be quite dramatic and devastating. Unfortunately, the structures of the Irish economy were undermined over recent years and policy-makers neglected to ensure that industries and jobs that could be sustained in the longer term would be nurtured. Ireland is now paying the price for this neglect and will continue to, unless policy is refocused on sustainable growth and economic activity.

Quality of Leadership

Before going into the above points in more detail, I want to take a look at the legacy of the leader who presided over the policy decisions during the period of the boom, Bertie Ahern. An analysis of his leadership and leadership in general is constructive as it allows some perspective on what Ireland wants and needs in her leaders in the future.

John Quincy Adams once said that 'If your actions inspire others to dream more, learn more, do more and become more, you are a leader.' This is particularly true for the leader of a country, who has to inspire and lead many different individuals from very different socio-economic backgrounds along the same path. In the context of the Irish economy and Irish society, there are many leaders at different levels of society. The taoiseach is obviously the person with most power, because he or she is elected to lead the people forward. For a taoiseach, the quality of the team that is put in place to help run the country is also vitally important, as is the quality of the public administration. A leader must be confident in his or her own ability and must not be afraid to put in place a team that may contain members who actually have more ability than themselves.

For a taoiseach, or indeed any leader, to be successful, characteristics such as charisma, bravery and vision are all essential attributes. President Obama in the US would appear to have those attributes in abundance, as did President Clinton. On the other hand, President George W. Bush did not. I was in the US when President Bush was sort of elected to the US presidency the first time around. Following the debacle with the election count in Florida, there was a palpable sense of a population that was less than enthusiastic about their new president and who could not believe that the workings of the physical electoral system could backfire so badly. US self-confidence took a serious battering in subsequent years. This battering was of course exacerbated by 9/11, the bursting of the dot-com bubble and the military adventures in Iraq and Afghanistan. But certainly President Bush did not inspire the population to follow or have faith in him. It is obviously too soon to judge Obama, and given the very partisan nature of the US political system his task will not be easy. However, there is certainly a sense in the US that they can start to dream more and do more. Effective leadership is key to this.

As mentioned in Chapter 2, Charles Haughey, Ray MacSharry and Alan Dukes provided strong leadership to the Irish people at a time of economic crisis in 1987. They took hard decisions that the electorate bought into, and this inspired the nation's confidence. That sort of inspirational leadership is lacking in Ireland at the moment. Despite expectations at the time of his elevation to taoiseach, and I certainly believed he would be a strong leader who would not be afraid to take hard decisions, Brian Cowen's leadership is not proving inspirational. The public perception is of a leader who has no vision for where he wants to take Ireland or, even if he has the vision, does not have the charisma to take the people with him. Despite this, it is clear that the generality of Irish people are still prepared to give him the benefit of the doubt and are almost willing him to become a strong and charismatic leader. In an interview with the *Sunday Independent*[4] in August 2009, Cowen got an opportunity to put things right. Certainly, from my perspective, I expected to see an interview where Cowen would lay out his vision for the country and articulate how he was going to make that vision become a reality. Instead, we got a series of banal quotes from him. For example, he stated that 'It's a great privilege to have the job' and that his attitude is 'to get on with it. It is what it is.' He went on to describe leadership as a requirement for the Cabinet to 'get out more, me included'. This was hardly the sort of inspirational rhetoric that a disillusioned population is looking for.

One of the depressing things about Ireland at the moment is that there is little in the way of real leadership in evidence across Irish society. The political system appears largely bereft of inspirational leaders, the moral authority of the Catholic Church has been seriously undermined, bankers are justifiably a very discredited bunch, and business interests in general are viewed with quite a bit of disdain by the population. There is, in my view, a dangerous leadership vacuum. The danger is that vacuums can be very easily filled by undesirable elements.

'Bertinomics'

When Bertie Ahern stepped down as taoiseach of Ireland in May 2008, the general consensus was that he had been one of the most successful premiers in Irish history. He had presided over the country from 1997 to 2008, a period that was characterised in the main by unprecedented levels of economic growth, strong employment creation and significant progress in relation to the Northern Ireland political situation. He was the second longest serving taoiseach in Ireland's history and led Fianna Fáil to three successive election victories in 1997, 2002 and 2007.

On the surface at least his economic and political legacy looks very strong. Few would argue with his political skills in bringing the different factions together in Northern Ireland, but there are serious question marks surrounding his economic legacy. Of course, Brian Cowen also has to take much responsibility for the evolution of the economy during Bertie's reign, because he was minister for finance from 2004 to 2008. However, the buck has to ultimately stop at the taoiseach because he is meant to be the one who is really in charge.

'Bertinomics' describes the flawed economic ideology of quantity over quality that controlled and directed Irish economic and social life over the period from 1997 to 2008 under Bertie Ahern's successive governments. To my way of thinking, the term describes a frightening level of economic illiteracy for which this and future generations will pay for years to come.

Unlike Cowen, Ahern had a charmed life as taoiseach. He led the country at a time when it would have been very difficult to blow it and left office before the real ordure hit the fan. Martin Luther King, Jr once said that 'The ultimate measure of a man is not where he stands in moments of comfort, but where he stands at times of challenge and controversy.' Bertie Ahern as taoiseach was never tested by very much in the way of challenge or controversy. His period in charge of the country could be an apt example of what Publilius Syrus said in the first century BC: 'Anyone can hold the helm when the sea is calm.' This was certainly the case with Ahern, who ruled Ireland at a time of very calm seas. However, we now know that he left quite a bit of pollution in those seas that his successor is struggling to clean up.

When asked whether he preferred brilliant generals or courageous generals, Napoleon famously answered that he preferred lucky generals to either of the other two varieties. As taoiseach of Ireland, Bertie Ahern certainly qualified as a lucky general rather than a brilliant or courageous one. In fact, it is difficult to identify much that was either courageous or brilliant in relation to his stewardship of the economy. It is difficult to find any evidence of Ahern ever making a hard decision during his period in office, and this culture of avoidance spread through his Government, who now seem to find it impossible to make any real decisions. This could be described as policy paralysis.

When he stepped down as taoiseach I wrote that Bertie Ahern would go down in Irish history as one of the worst leaders Ireland ever had from an economic and financial perspective, and I marked his leaving office with the suggestion, 'Bertie, it could have been so much better.' This was not intended as a political jibe, but rather reflected my sense of frustration, disillusionment and despondency that, after a decade of such strong economic growth, our economy and society were still characterised by so many imbalances and shortcomings. Given the amount of money that was generated in tax revenues over his period in office, it is a real pity that the money was not used in a more prudent manner and that the economy was not managed with the long term in mind. This is already starting to exert a heavy price on the social and commercial life of the country.

Now, in leaner times, there is a strong sense that a major opportunity was missed to put Ireland into the premier division in terms of infrastructure, public services and general quality of life. Bertie Ahern and his various governments must take much of the responsibility for these failures, but there is, to date, little evidence that this is actually happening or indeed likely to happen. Bertie Ahern still appears to believe that his economic legacy is a positive one, while those who surrounded him in government are still to the fore in Irish life and have a level of smugness and arrogance that is hard to stomach. Everybody is being blamed for the mess the country is now in except themselves. Such is the way of politics, particularly politics of the Irish variety.

The headline economic facts during Ahern's tenure are indeed impressive. GDP experienced annual average growth of 7.2 per cent between 1997 and 2007. To put this in context, GDP growth in the Euro Zone averaged 2.2 per cent over that period, and Ireland had averaged 2.4 per cent growth during the 1980s. The unemployment rate fell from 10.3 per cent of the labour force in 1997 to 4.6 per cent at the end of 2007 and total employment in the economy increased from 1.4 million to 2.1 million.[5] This is all very impressive on the surface at least. However, as discussed, there are serious question marks over the quality and sustainability of what was achieved.

The fact is that, particularly in his first term in office from 1997 to 2002, Ahern was a major beneficiary of policies that had been put in place by some of his predecessors. As discussed in Chapter 2, the elements that contributed to the creation of the boom, such as the favourable corporation tax regime, the availability of a young, well-educated and English-speaking labour force and foreign direct investment, were the products of previous policy-making.

However, the real legacy of Bertie Ahern's period in office is only now starting to resonate with the Irish population. There is general recognition that the timing of his leaving office was extremely fortuitous. Since May 2008, a bank guarantee scheme has had to be put in place, Anglo Irish Bank has been nationalised, the whole domestic banking system has been re-capitalised using taxpayers' hard-earned money, tax revenues have collapsed and 221,800 people have been forced to join the live register. The international reputation of Ireland has been seriously damaged by failures of regulation, corporate governance, and economic and financial collapse. Is it the case that Brian Lenihan and Brian Cowen are basically incompetent and managed to take a successful economy and turn it into a total mess over a period of fifteen months, or is there some other explanation? Brian Lenihan and Brian Cowen are not incompetent and, try as they might, it would be impossible for virtually anybody to damage an economy to the extent that the Irish economy has been damaged over such a relatively short period of time. The truth is that both men were handed a bucket of the proverbial by Bertie Ahern.

The situation had already turned around by the time Ahern stepped down, but he was not prepared to admit it. The housing market had been declining since February 2007, as had the Irish equity market; the number of people signing on the dole had increased by 35,000 over the previous twelve months; and the public finances were already under significant pressure as tax revenues collapsed. Ahern's Government up to the point of his departure either refused or were unable to comprehend the fact that the economy was in big trouble. As mentioned, anybody who dared suggest that things were not as they appeared got short shrift. Addressing an Irish Congress of Trade Unions (ICTU) conference in Donegal in July 2007, Ahern said that 'Sitting on the sidelines, cribbing and moaning is a lost opportunity. I don't know how people who engage in that don't commit suicide because frankly the only thing that motivates me is being able to actively change something.' This comment elicited a very negative reaction from suicide groups and many others and he later apologised. As it happens, his unfortunate choice of expression has become cruelly ironic, since over the last couple of years a number of suicides have been reported that were at least partly down to the changed economic and financial climate.

In his last couple of years in office Ahern was clearly more preoccupied with defending his honour in a fairytale fashion at the Mahon Tribunal in Dublin Castle, while many of his colleagues were back in the Dáil defending him. The pity is that the eye was taken off the ball during a crucial period and early remedial action to at least partly correct the evolving situation was not taken. By the time the Government cottoned on to the fact that there was a deep crisis, it was too late.

In assessing the economic legacy of Bertie Ahern during his tenure as taoiseach, it is difficult to know where to start or where to finish. Such a negative assessment of Ahern's period in office might appear strange and unfair in the context of a leader who had presided over such an incredible economic boom. But the reality is that we are all now being forced to take the pain involved in cleaning up the mess that was allowed develop. As taoiseach, it should have been the responsibility of Ahern and his Cabinet to manage the economy in a more prudent manner, but this did not happen. Bertie Ahern cannot be blamed for all of Ireland's current economic and financial ills, but as leader of the country he has to take a huge amount of responsibility. That is what real leadership should be about.

The following chapters (4–6) look at the policies of Bertie Ahern's Governments and how they led Ireland into the current undesirable economic situation.

4

Creating a One-Winged Bird

History shows that it is the nature of any bubble, but particularly in real estate, that it creates a 'bubble mentality': a belief that prices cannot go down and that borrowing or lending on the security of houses is a safe investment. It was this belief, both driver of and driven by the credit bubble, which inflated house prices to extraordinary highs. When they crashed back down, the world financial system and the world economy were standing underneath.
John P. Calverley, *When Bubbles Burst*, 2009

In 2002 I was hosting some German business visitors to Dublin. We were in a high building looking out over the Dublin skyline, when one of them commented in an understated German fashion that 'Ze crane is clearly ze national bird of Ireland.' Although I hadn't really noticed it until then, the Dublin skyline at that stage was indeed dominated by cranes of all shapes and sizes. Since that experience with the observant German, 'counting the cranes' was one piece of anecdotal economic research that I utilised as I went about the dark art of economic forecasting.

If the Celtic Tiger was a phenomenon based on foreign direct investment and an export boom, the economy of the noughties was undoubtedly a phenomenon based on a dramatic construction boom. A 'crane count' in Dublin at the moment, or indeed in any part of the country, paints a very different picture than during the peak of the construction madness.

As we know, Ireland got caught up in an unprecedented construction boom over the past decade, particularly in the residential market. The market for both builders and buyers became totally euphoric and rationality was thrown out the window. Looking back on some of what I wrote during that period does cause me to blush somewhat, but then again that is one of the hazards of putting one's thoughts into print. In November 2005 I wrote:

> Demand for housing remains very strong and continues to be driven by low mortgage rates, strong employment growth, record levels of inward migration, and generally supportive demographics. All of these factors are set to remain influential and the market remains soundly based and is gradually moving towards a soft landing. The risks of a hard landing are still very low. In overall terms, the latest readings on the market suggest that, while house price growth is on a long-term decelerating trend, the market still remains very solid. National average house prices are set to grow by 8 per cent this year [2005] and by around 5 per cent in 2006.[1]

As suggested in this piece, I believed at that stage that Irish house prices were beginning a process of softening and that this would reduce the prospect of a hard landing occurring at some later stage. This forecast was based on a view that the evolution of prices to that point could be broadly justified by fundamentals, but that these fundamentals were now suggesting that an easing of prices would be appropriate. Furthermore, the interest rate cycle was starting to turn. Alas, how wrong can one be?

The Irish housing market in the first half of 2006 went totally berserk. A sort of manic panic set in during that period. Every week we were hit with headlines of auction results in the press declaring houses at auction achieving up to 50 per cent above the asking price. In the six months to the end of June 2006, national average house prices, as measured by the Permanent TSB/ESRI house price index, had increased by almost 8 per cent and by almost 12 per cent by the end of that year. So much for house price forecasts! I concluded at that stage that I did not really understand the dynamics of the Irish housing market, and I threw my hands in the air and decided to go with the trend. Of course, I missed the turn in the market when it eventually occurred in the early months of 2007. I still believe, however, that the market activity in the first half of 2006 was what really drove the Irish housing market into serious bubble territory and beyond the realm of what could be explained by an examination of economic fundamentals. Unfortunately, this set the scene for the collapse in prices that occurred in 2008 and 2009.

The Economic Contribution of the Construction Sector

An accusation that is often thrown at Fianna Fáil by critics of the party relates to the incredibly strong links between that party and the construction industry. Prior to Brian Cowen shutting it down, the Fianna Fáil tent at the annual race meeting in Galway every July bore testament to this accusation. The tent was always full of builders and developers who wanted to rub shoulders with and make financial contributions to the party. Perhaps if somebody else had been in government it would have been no different, but the fact is that Fianna Fáil is normally in government and so it has always been worthwhile for builders and developers to build up a good relationship with the power brokers in the party.

This close relationship has not been good for the Irish economy as it played no small part in the creation of the construction bubble that is now causing so many problems for the Irish financial system and the economy in general. Arguably, the biggest indictment of Irish economic policy-making over the past decade was the policy of promoting as much construction activity as possible all over the country and ensuring that the banking system lent money to builders and developers in an imprudent and reckless manner. We are all now paying the price for this folly and will continue to do so for generations to come. The inordinate dependence on construction activity that was allowed develop is the best or worst example of how quality was sacrificed to quantity. As long as the construction sector was throwing out so many positive economic returns, nobody that 'mattered' ever questioned if this was sensible or indeed sustainable.

At the peak of the construction boom in 2007, the following were the facts relating to the construction industry:

- Total output from the construction sector was valued at €38.5 billion, equivalent to over 20 per cent of GDP
- The value of residential house building was put at €22.7 billion, equivalent to 12 per cent of GDP[2]
- Between 2002 and 2007, 455,871 new housing units were completed, compared to 135,018 between 1992 and 1997.[3]

Construction- and housing-related activity became a major driver of Exchequer tax revenues at the peak of the boom. Tax receipts came in directly through stamp duties, VAT on new housing and capital gains tax. The indirect tax sources were income tax on employment, corporation tax from companies operating in construction and related activities, and tax receipts related to consumer spending directly flowing from the high employment in the industry. In 2006, stamp duty receipts relating to land and property transactions totalled just under €3 billion, which was equivalent to over 80 per cent of total receipts from stamp duties. In 2007, the total stamp duty take from land- and property-related transactions was €2.38 billion, equivalent to 73 per cent of total receipts from stamp duties. The VAT take on new housing in 2006 is estimated at around €3.3 billion and at around €3.7 billion in 2007.[4] It is estimated that the total tax take for the Exchequer from every new house is 40 per cent of the price of the house excluding VAT. This means that the total tax take from new housing in 2006 was around €9.8 billion and around €11.1 billion in 2007. The total tax take for the Exchequer in 2006 was €45 billion and €47 billion in 2007.[5] It is clear from this analysis that construction and related activities had become the key driver of tax revenues in the economy by 2007.

In its annual report in 2008, the Revenue Commissioners stated that, in relation to the shortfall of receipts from stamp duties, which came in over a billion behind expectations in 2008, 'some 87 per cent of the shortfall from stamp duties in 2008 was attributable to lower than expected returns from property transactions (of all types) in terms of both diminished property values and reduced numbers of transactions.' In relation to receipts from capital gains tax, which came in €1.8 billion behind target, the Revenue Commissioners stated that 'the shortfall is attributable to the downturn in the property and share markets', and likewise in relation to VAT receipts. Quite literally, the massive deterioration in the Irish public finance situation in 2008 and 2009 was primarily attributable to the bursting of the construction bubble.

The construction sector also became a major employer and driver of employment in the Irish economy during the period of the construction boom. At the peak of the cycle in 2007, the construction sector accounted for 13.5 per cent of total employment in the Irish economy. Indeed, in the first quarter of 2007, the construction sector accounted for almost 14.5 per cent of total employment in the Irish economy. The EU average was around 5 per cent at that stage. Ireland built up a labour market dependence on the construction sector that was almost three times greater than the EU average. There was always the inevitability that at some stage Ireland would start to converge on the EU average. That is now happening at an alarming pace.

Table 2 examines the change in total employment in the Irish economy between 2002 and 2007, which is really the period that covers the peak of the property and construction boom. Of the total employment created in the economy between 2002 and 2007, the construction sector was the biggest driver, accounting for 29.5 per cent of total employment in the economy. Between January 2002 and December 2007, the value of outstanding mortgages in the economy expanded from €34 billion to just under €140 billion.[6] This is a dramatic increase by any stretch of the imagination. Clearly, housing-related activity also became a key driver of

**Table 2: Change in Total Employment in the Irish Economy
2002–2007**

Sector	Change 2002–2007	% Contribution
Agriculture, Forestry & Fishing	-9,600	-2.8%
Other Production	-9,200	-2.7%
Construction	+100,700	+29.5%
Wholesale & Retail Trade	+48,900	+14.3%
Hotels & Restaurants	+26,300	+7.7%
Transport, Storage & Communication	+11,200	+3.3%
Financial & Other Business Services	+56,800	+16.7%
Public Administration & Defence	+12,100	+3.5%
Education	+28,800	+8.4%
Health	+53,600	+15.7%
Other Services	+21,400	+6.4%
Total	**+341,000**	**100.0%**

Source: CSO, *Quarterly National Household Survey.*

employment in the financial services sector and in related legal and other services, such as conveyancing.

The Irish equity market by 2006 had become heavily influenced by and dependent on the health of the housing market and housing-related activities. The main companies with the heaviest exposure at that stage were Allied Irish Banks, Bank of Ireland, Anglo Irish Bank, Irish Life & Permanent, Grafton Group, Abbey, IFG Group, Kingspan Group, McInerney Holdings, Readymix and, to a limited extent, CRH. On the back of the housing and mortgage boom from 2002 onwards, the Irish equity market performed very strongly, with the index increasing by 284 per cent between March 2002 and the peak of the Irish equity market in February 2007.[7] The Irish equity market peaked in February 2007, and by March 2009 it had lost over 80 per cent of its value, with the banking stocks in particular faring considerably worse. Bank of Ireland's share price lost over 99 per cent of its value between the peak in February 2007 and the trough in March 2009. Allied Irish Banks lost just less than 99 per cent of its value over the same period.[8] It is interesting that the Irish equity market and the banking stocks peaked in the same month as the Irish housing market, and they both subsequently sank together.

In 2007, the Irish housing market was worth in excess of €550 billion, which is more than three times the level of national income. This is a massive amount of personal wealth tied up in housing. Given the high level of home ownership in Ireland and the rapid increase in the value of housing stock over the period of the boom, the fortunes of the market had a considerable impact on consumer confidence and consumer spending. Real growth in consumer spending averaged just over 5 per cent per annum,[9] which does represent strong growth by any definition of the word. The spending binge was pretty widespread, with particularly strong increases in spending on furniture and household fittings to kit out the thousands of new homes that were being built. Car sales also featured strongly. Between 2002 and 2007, 963,409 new private motor cars were licensed for the first time. In the period from 1992 to 1997, the total was 524,307.[10] The total credit card spend in 2002 was €7.3 billion,[11] but this increased to €14 billion in 2007. Not surprisingly, employment in the wholesale and retail trade sector increased by 48,900, accounting for 14.3 per cent of total jobs created in the economy over the period.[12] Also not surprisingly, the indebtedness of the personal sector increased quite dramatically. Outstanding mortgage credit increased from €34 billion at the end of 2001 to almost €140 billion by the end of 2007. Other non-mortgage personal borrowing increased from €8.3 billion in the middle of 2000 to €24.3 billion at the end of 2007.[13]

During this period, Ireland certainly put itself on the international map as a haven for consumers and retailers. This was reflected in a surge in foreign retailers coming into the country to exploit the consumer nirvana. Indeed, Bus Éireann put on a special bus service to facilitate those Irish consumers who wished to travel north of the border to shop in IKEA, before IKEA opened in Dublin.

As house prices increased over the boom period, consumers borrowed and spent on the strength of the rising housing market. Since the housing market started to go into decline in February 2007, we have seen the other side of the coin – namely a very negative consumer wealth effect which has seriously undermined consumer confidence and consumer spending power.

In March 2006 I published a report[14] analysing the extent to which the housing market had become the key driver of the Irish economy, with its influence felt very strongly in employment in construction, financial services and the housing-related retail sectors, in Exchequer tax receipts, in consumer sentiment and spending power, and in the Irish equity market. I pointed out that any significant setback to the housing market, either through prices falling sharply or house building activity contracting, would seriously undermine the economy. I went on to argue that house building could not continue at the pace evident at that stage and that policy-makers needed to ensure that a sustainable indigenous economy was developed in parallel with the construction-driven economy in order to take up the slack should the housing market go into reverse. This was not in any way inspired analysis, but was merely a statement of the obvious. I went on to consider the implications of a 20 per cent decline in house prices, and concluded that a correction of such magnitude would have a significant impact on the overall economy. In no way did I envisage the extent to which the housing market would eventually correct in both price and activity terms. My analysis was too conservative, but in the midst of the insanity that gripped the housing market in the early months of 2006, it certainly did not feel that way. It is very easy to be wise in hindsight.

Creating a Housing Bubble: The Fundamentals that Drove the Market

The trend in Irish house prices over the past decade has been quite dramatic by any standards. Between December 1996 and the peak of the market in February 2007, national average house prices increased by 290 per cent according to the Permanent TSB/ESRI index. Over the same period, average consumer prices, as measured by the Consumer Price Index (CPI), increased by just 40.4 per cent.

That house price inflation should exceed general inflation in the economy to such a dramatic extent is quite amazing and on the surface it suggests that, even prior to 2006, the market had lost the run of itself. However, that is not quite the case. In the decade between 1985 and 1995 the Irish housing market had been pretty lacklustre. Between 1985 and 1995 national average house prices had increased by around 65 per cent, while consumer price inflation had increased by just over 40 per cent over the same period. This is not exactly the stuff of speculative bubbles. Prior to the market taking off in the late 1990s, Irish house prices were relatively low and there was certainly an element of catch-up thereafter, but unfortunately the catch-up process proved too aggressive and eventually created a very dangerous situation.

The relatively lacklustre housing market performance over the decade up to 1995 really reflected the poor economic background, high interest rates over much of the period, a serious lack of confidence in the economy and a mortgage market where there was not much in the way of competition. This led to high mortgage margins, limited mortgage product innovation and constrained credit availability.

All of this changed utterly in the second half of the 1990s when a number of factors combined to push the housing market into a different sphere. These included the general transformation of the economy and the labour market, the dramatic turnaround in Ireland's migratory patterns, the collapse in interest rates, increased competition in the marketplace and a number of structural factors.

Economic Transformation

Between 1995 and 2007 annual economic growth averaged 7.5 per cent. On the back of this growth, the labour market was transformed in a dramatic fashion. The number of people in full-time employment increased from 1.3 million to 2.1 million and the unemployment rate declined from 12.2 per cent to just 4.4 per cent in the early months of 2007.[15] Another feature of that economic transformation was the fact that strong growth in wages combined with the steady easing of the personal tax burden to deliver significant growth in disposable incomes. Personal disposable incomes increased by almost 170 per cent between 1995 and 2006.

Not terribly surprisingly, in an environment of virtual full employment, unprecedented economic buoyancy and massive growth in disposables incomes, the demand for housing picked up very strongly.

Migration and Demographic Factors

In conjunction with and partly as a result of the economic transformation, migratory flows also altered significantly during those years. Between 1995 and 2007 there was net inward migration of 416,000 people.[16] Over the same period, there was a natural increase (i.e. the total number of births exceeding the number of deaths) of 344,000 in the population. Due to both of these factors, the population increased by 760,000 or by more than 21 per cent over that decade.[17] As well as the strong growth in population, the age profile of the population is also very young. At the time of the 2006 census, almost 25 per cent of the Irish population was aged between 25 and 39 years; in other words, there were just over 1 million people in the particular age segment of the population where household formation typically occurs and where people tend to buy their first house.

Structural Factors

In addition to the growth in population from domestic and external sources, and the large segment of the population in the household formation age group, a number of structural developments in the Irish demographic profile also fuelled demand for housing. These factors included an increase in the number of double-income households, higher divorce rates and a sharp fall in household size.

On 24 November 1995 over 1 million Irish voters decided in favour of lifting the ban on divorce in Ireland, which had been introduced by Eamon De Valera in his 1937 Constitution. Divorce became available for the first time in February 1997 when the Family Law (Divorce) Act became law. At the time of the 2006 census there were 59,500 divorced persons living in Ireland and 107,300 separated persons. This rise in marriage breakups was undoubtedly another contributor to the increase in demand for housing.

The sharp fall in average household size has also had an influence on the demand for housing. Back in the 1920s, the typical Irish house was quite crowded, with an average of 4.48 people occupying it.[18] By 1996, 3.14 people lived in the average Irish house and at the time of the 2006 census this had fallen to 2.81 persons. A few factors pushing down this number is falling family size and growth in the number of one-person households. Between 1996 and 2006 the number of one-person households increased from 241,800 to 329,500.[19] This could possibly reflect an increasingly isolated and anti-social product of the Celtic Tiger – better to live on one's own than to share the bounty of the new economic reality with others! Whatever the reason, population increase combined with falling household size caused a significant rise in demand for housing.

Interest Rates and Financial Market Deregulation

The aforementioned economic, demographic and other structural factors clearly gave a major boost to housing demand, but the biggest contributors were the dramatic changes in the cost of mortgages and in the very fabric of the mortgage industry

As well as having one of the highest levels of home ownership in the developed world, Irish mortgage borrowers typically tend to opt for variable mortgage interest rates or short-period fixed-rate products. One reason for this is that many mortgage holders who had opted for fixed-rate products in the past discovered that they would have been better off on variable rates. Many fail to understand that opting for a fixed-rate mortgage is an insurance policy that will allow you to sleep at night and also gives you certainty in financial planning and household budgeting. However, there tends to be a basic mistrust of financial institutions in Ireland, much of it well deserved it has to be said; many cynical mortgage holders and indeed other bank customers tend to work on the basis that, if a financial institution is trying to flog a certain product, then it must be for the benefit of the institution rather than the customer. It is difficult to argue with that notion.

In any event, at the end of 2008, almost 80 per cent of outstanding mortgages in the Irish market were variable rate mortgages, while just over 2 per cent of total mortgages outstanding were fixed for a period of more than five years. The proportion of mortgage holders on variable rates was somewhat higher than normal at the end of 2008 due to the exceptionally low interest rate environment that the European Central Bank (ECB) delivered in response to the global economic crisis. However, variable rates have always played a dominant role in the Irish mortgage market. The result of this is that the Irish mortgage market tends to be sensitive to trends in short-term interest rates.

Irish short-term interest rates experienced a once-off step adjustment in the second half of the 1990s. In a single currency area, there is a common short-term interest rate between participant countries, so in the run up to the beginning of the EMU and the creation of the single European currency in 1999, Irish short-term interest rates fell sharply as they converged on traditionally lower German interest rate levels. At the end of 1992 the three-month interbank interest rate in Dublin stood at 17.5 per cent, compared to an equivalent German rate of 8.7 per cent. However, by the end of 1999, this had fallen to 3.3 per cent and to just over 2 per cent by the middle of 2005.[20] Irish variable rate borrowers enjoyed a bonanza of unprecedented proportions from this collapse in interest rates and they reacted accordingly. The new interest rate environment allowed them to take on bigger and bigger mortgages, which they did with gay abandon. This in turn led to them paying higher and higher prices for housing.

Credit was not only cheaper but the supply of credit in the Irish market also increased dramatically. There was a time in the not-too-distant past when the Irish mortgage market was dominated by the building societies and this oligopolistic position allowed them to be very choosy about to whom they would grant a mortgage. In reality, you almost had to get down on your knees and beg for a mortgage in the 1980s and, if you managed to get one, you were indeed privileged. Despite having a relatively secure and pensionable job in the mid-1980s, I had to doctor my earnings position and beg profusely to obtain my first mortgage from a building society. This all changed dramatically in the late 1990s, as deregulation and the advent of the euro allowed new domestic and foreign players to enter the market.

By the middle of 2008 there were eighteen residential mortgage providers in the Irish market. One might be tempted to suggest that a market the size of Ireland's could not justify eighteen providers, but at the peak of the mortgage boom everybody wanted a slice of the lucrative action. Some of the eighteen never had anything other than an extremely small or geographically remote presence in the market via the Internet, and the reality is that it continued to be dominated by a small number of players. Despite this, the market did become increasingly competitive.

As we enter 2010, it was hard to say how many providers were still really in the market because, although many of them have a physical or Internet presence, they are not really open for business due to a combination of the global credit crunch and the toxic nature of the seriously injured Irish mortgage market. The foreign-owned institutions in particular are not very active because the parent companies have become increasingly sceptical about the Irish market and are not prepared to allocate capital to their Irish operations. They have learned a valuable lesson, albeit a bit too late.

Going back to 1999, the advent of the single European currency fundamentally altered the nature of the Irish mortgage market. With the opening up of European financial markets and the elimination of exchange rate risk, Irish banks increasingly gained access to wholesale money markets. Faced with unprecedented growth in mortgage demand, the financial institutions increasingly funded their operations in international wholesale money markets because the customer deposit base was simply not large enough to satisfy their new-found ambitions. The net external liabilities of Irish credit institutions increased from €9 billion at the end of 1999 to €108 billion at the end of 2007.[21] This was exaggerated by the IFSC banks, but the message is clear.

This access to international wholesale funding enabled rapid growth in mortgage lending and banks effectively forgot they were banks and became primarily mortgage lenders. Despite its very small size, Celtic Tiger Ireland, as a member of the Euro Zone, really put itself on the map to an extent that was totally unprecedented and not really warranted. Ireland was now punching well above its financial weight and international banks were prepared to invest in the covered bonds and securities issued by the Irish banks; these international banks effectively came to finance the runaway growth in Irish mortgage lending after 2000.

Apart from entry into the Euro Zone, the other most significant development in the recent history of the Irish mortgage market was undoubtedly the entry of Bank of Scotland (BoS) in September 1999. BoS was introduced to the Irish market by brokers and began life by offering a variable rate mortgage of 3.69 per cent, which compared to an average variable rate mortgage of 5.17 per cent at this time. Before its entry, the differential between the ECB's official interest rate and the variable rate mortgage stood at 2.86 per cent. BoS made a price pledge not to charge a differential of more than 1.5 per cent above the ECB official rate. By December 1999, just three months after the new entrant arrived, the differential between the average variable rate mortgage available in the market and the ECB rate had narrowed to just 1.14 per cent. BoS spotted an anomaly in the market in the shape of a very attractive margin, and forced the existing players in the market to respond. This they did, and the net result was that the cost of mortgage finance to the customer experienced another once-off downward adjustment or step change.

BoS was also the first institution to introduce the concept of the 'tracker mortgage' to the traditionally conservative Irish market. A tracker mortgage is a mortgage product that charges a fixed rate over the ECB's base interest rate. Very quickly other banks followed suit and the tracker product became popular, with institutions typically offering a fixed margin of less than 1 per cent over the ECB base rate. However, the tracker concept was blown out of the water when, in 2007, the cost of funding for banks on wholesale markets increased significantly due to the global credit crisis. At that stage, trackers became very unprofitable for the providers as they were forced to pay well above the ECB base rate for funding in the market, and by the middle of 2009 the product had become virtually extinct, apart from those that were already in existence prior to the outbreak of volatility in the money markets.

Apart from the introduction of the tracker mortgage, BoS really shook up the Irish mortgage market and, although it did not gain much in terms of market share at least early on, it forced competitors to react and effectively revolutionised the marketplace. Bank of Scotland's entry into the market was the beginning of a process that ultimately resulted in the Irish mortgage market becoming a seriously competitive market characterised by lots of 'innovation', as the various providers reacted to the new environment by introducing a host of products and initiatives that resulted in a surge in cheap credit. Some further examples of this 'innovation' include equity release products, higher loan-to-value (LTV) mortgages, interest-only mortgages and the mortgage chequebook.

Equity is basically the value one builds up in one's house over and above the level of the mortgage. Over the period of the real house price boom between 1995 and 2006, for many people the value of their property increased way above the value of their outstanding mortgage. This was particularly the case for older people who often had very small mortgages or, in many cases, no mortgage at all. People such as these often lived in a very valuable asset but had serious income constraints. The 'innovative' bankers decided to target such people and allow them borrow on the strength of the equity built up in their home. In 2001, Bank of Ireland introduced the 'Life Loan', which was aimed at the 'asset rich, cash poor' over-65 age segment of the market. Customers were allowed borrow up to 30 per cent of the value of their home at a fixed but high rate for the first fifteen years, and at the end of that period they could choose either a new fixed rate or a variable rate. This was a tad bizarre, given the strong probability that mortality would have caught up with someone over 65 after fifteen years, but that is the nature of financial innovation. The funds borrowed were typically used to pay for medical expenses and essential home improvements, and no repayments would be made until the maturity of the loan. Many other providers introduced similar equity release-type products. While they may have looked well in a rising house price environment, in a rapidly falling price environment they might not look quite as attractive.

In the past, conservative bankers would rarely lend more than 80 per cent of the value of the property, but in an environment of rapidly rising house prices and increased competition in the marketplace, mortgage providers started to offer 100 per cent LTV mortgages and there were even cases where a higher LTV loan could be acquired. It is a bit of a chicken and egg situation. On the one hand, one could argue that higher LTV loans allowed sound borrowing propositions the opportunity to buy the more expensive property that they desired. On the other hand, however, one could argue that giving the borrower more money just drove the price higher. I would be inclined to argue for the latter rather than the former. In 2004, just 5 per cent of mortgages issued had an LTV of 100 per cent, but this had jumped to 12 per cent by 2007. In 2006, 33 per cent of mortgages given out had an LTV in excess of 91 per cent.[22] These high LTVs have created serious problems for up to 300,000 borrowers, who by the middle of 2009 find themselves in the undesirable position of negative equity. Negative equity will take some years to work out of the system. At one level, negative equity is not the end of the world unless one is forced to sell one's house, but unfortunately that is now happening to many people as unemployment rises, just as happened in the UK in the 1980s. Even if one is not forced to sell, it is pretty soul-destroying for anybody to realise that they have a mortgage that is much bigger than it should be and which they will be paying back for years to come. The existence of negative equity is also likely to put pressure on consumer spending. Little wonder that the electorate gave the Government such a kicking in the mid-2009 elections because, regardless of whose fault it is, Government will always tend to get the blame.

In September 2002, Permanent TSB introduced a cheque-book mortgage called OnePlan. This product was aimed at somebody who was typically more than four years into the mortgage and who would have built up some equity in their property. OnePlan allowed the borrower to release equity from €40,000 up to a maximum of 85 per cent of the current market value of the property less the amount owed on the mortgage. For people who chose the OnePlan variable rate product, they could immediately get a cheque for the full amount borrowed. If you did not want access to all of the funds immediately, you had the option of using a OnePlan mortgage chequebook to pay for whatever purchases you wanted to make, subject to the condition that the minimum cheque withdrawal was €3,000. The marketing blurb on the OnePlan product stated:

> You've always said 'one day' you'll get that new kitchen or conservatory, buy that holiday home or take the trip of a lifetime. As a Permanent TSB customer you can now make 'one day' today with OnePlan from Permanent TSB. OnePlan is a great way to borrow money based on the hidden equity, or value, in your home or in your investment property.

Incidentally, at the time this product was launched I had a heated debate with the head of marketing at Permanent TSB on the *Last Word* on Today FM, which was presented at the time by Eamon Dunphy. I could not understand or believe that such a product could be launched or that it would not create potential for serious problems down the road. The notion that somebody could pay for a holiday by signing a cheque drawn on their mortgage account and pay it back over 30 years did strike me as being strange. My opponent disagreed with this view. I am not sure who won that particular argument or who has been proven correct.

Another significant development in the market was the pressure brought to bear and the inducements offered to mortgage holders to switch their mortgage to another lender. Some mortgage providers offered lump sums and the payment of all legal costs to customers of other institutions to switch their mortgage. By 2007, the level of switching was worth €6.7 billion, equivalent to almost 20 per cent of the mortgage market. In the second quarter of 2009 the total was just €330 million.[23]

The average length of the mortgage has also been pushed out considerably in the face of rapidly rising house prices. To pay the high asking prices, borrowers had to borrow for longer and longer periods of time in order to be able to afford the monthly repayments. In 2004, just 10 per cent of mortgages drawn down were for periods in excess of 31 years, but by 2007 this had jumped to 35 per cent of mortgages. In 2007, 2 per cent of mortgages were for terms in excess of 36 years.[24] Not alone were people being forced to take bigger and bigger mortgages, but they would be saddled with them for the rest of their working lives and beyond.

Lenders also relaxed their lending criteria in the face of intense competition and strong demand for mortgages. There was a time when lenders were prepared to lend two-and-a-half times the salary of the primary earner plus the salary of the second earner. Interest-only loans were not available at that stage and, for LTVs in excess of maybe 90 per cent, a mortgage indemnity bond or, in other words, a type of mortgage insurance was required for the percentage of the mortgage above a certain LTV level. The income multiples were politely discarded and borrowers started to think more in terms of the percentage of net income that would be needed to make the monthly mortgage repayments. At the same time, interest-only mortgages were introduced where only interest payments and no capital repayments would be required for maybe the first five years of the mortgage. Almost 13 per cent of total mortgages paid out in 2006 were interest-only. Some of these borrowers could be facing serious difficulties when they come off interest-only and have to start making capital repayments.

The aforementioned are just some of the examples of competition and 'innovation' in the mortgage market, but there are numerous variations on this general theme. The bottom line is that, at the peak of the housing market boom, mortgage providers were falling over each other to win new business or entice existing business away from other mortgage providers. Cheap and easy access to credit became the order of the day and people were encouraged to borrow aggressively to buy property regardless of the price or value, and others were encouraged and cajoled to release equity in their homes to fund their lifestyles. It certainly had become a buyer's market in the sense that getting access to credit was not a problem, to put it mildly, and mortgage providers were bending over backwards to facilitate the purchase of a house. On the negative side, house prices started to grow strongly. At the peak of the market in March 2006, the growth rate in net mortgage lending reached a staggering 28.1 per cent.[25] Somewhere in the dim and distant past I was told that there was an old-fashioned rule of thumb to the effect that credit growth should not exceed nominal growth in the economy for long. Nominal growth in the economy in 2006 was under 10 per cent, which was a far cry from the growth in mortgage credit the same year. It was indeed heady stuff.

The Role of the Investor

The property investor also made a strong contribution to the surge in demand for housing. The Irish have always had a preoccupation with bricks and mortar and the first thing most of us want to do when we start work is to buy our own house. Perhaps this is due to a desire to have privacy in pursuit of our nocturnal activities, but it is more probably born from the sense of security afforded by owning our own property. At the peak of the Celtic Tiger and subsequently, not alone did we want to own the property we lived in, we also wanted to own numerous other investment properties both at home and abroad. Fiscal incentives were offered to investors through various tax reliefs in certain designated areas, and they were also allowed to write off for tax purposes mortgage interest payments on the investment property against the rental income earned from the property.

Tax breaks for rental income were removed in 1998, but they were re-introduced in Budget 2002 by the then Minister for Finance Charlie McCreevy, on the basis that the presence of investors in the market was required to secure the future supply of housing to meet accommodation needs. House price inflation had slowed sharply during 2001 to just 4.4 per cent as Ireland suffered from the effects of the dot-com bust.[26] This slowdown in house prices was not an undesirable development, but, following the re-introduction of mortgage interest relief for investors, the market took off again in 2002 and by the end of that year prices had increased by over 13 per cent.[27] A couple of days after the change in Budget 2002 I was speaking at a Chamber of Commerce lunch in Dungarvan, County Waterford, where an auctioneer told me that, within hours of the change, investors were again beating down his door.

Apart from some sort of difficult-to-explain cultural affinity to bricks and mortar, Irish investors invested heavily in residential property on the basis of tax breaks, rental income, and, most importantly, a belief that capital values would continue to rise forever. At the peak of the mortgage market in 2006, investors borrowed €7.95 billion. This eased back to €6.5 billion in 2007 and just €4.1 billion in 2008. In the second quarter of 2009, the total lent to investors was a paltry €226 million.[28] The Irish love affair with property has ended due to a collapse in house prices, a realisation that capital values would not rise forever, falling rents and a lack of credit availability. Given the Irish predilection for property, one might be foolish to suggest that the love affair has finally run its course, but certainly for the moment the affair is very much on the rocks.

Another interesting feature of Irish property investor behaviour is the fact that they have diversified out of Ireland in recent years. The Irish investor has now colonised markets such as the UK, Germany, France, Spain and Portugal, but has also moved much further afield to places such as the US, Cape Verde, India, Brazil, Bulgaria, Romania and South Africa. It remains to be seen how these investments will pan out, but it is quite incredible to see Irish farmers using the family farm as security for apartment blocks in places like Berlin, and taxi drivers owning apartments in Bulgaria. That is only the tip of the iceberg. Unwittingly, I once commented at a debate in Cork that the notion of Irish investors moving into places such as Cape Verde was lunacy, only to discover that the hosts of the debate were one of the big promoters of Cape Verdean property in the south west.

I fervently believe that an awful lot of the property investments undertaken by Irish amateur investors overseas will turn out to be lunacy. Figures from CBRE Gunne suggest that the Irish property investment spend overseas in 2007 was €12.2 billion, up from €11.9 billion the previous year. If you had wanted a lesson in geography over the years, you would have needed to look no further than the property supplements in newspapers every Sunday to discover the latest 'hot spot'.

On top of all of the aforementioned factors driving housing demand, Ireland also has the most generous tax provisions for owner-occupied housing in the EU. Mortgage interest relief is available for owner-occupiers, although that is now being scaled back. However, it is still very generous for first-time buyers. Capital gains tax is not charged on the principle private residence, and imputed rent is not taxed. Up until recently, the only property tax was a stamp duty for some buyers at the time of purchase. In the Supplementary Budget of April 2009, the Government introduced a €200 annual tax on a second home.

The Supply Side

A combination of the above factors fuelled very strong demand in the housing market and, at least initially, supply was relatively slow to respond. Between 1990 and 1995, 140,484 houses were built in Ireland. In the period from 1996 to 2000, this jumped to 211,240 houses, but, in the period from 2001 to 2008, new house completions totalled 560,197. At the peak of the house building boom in 2006, 93,419 houses were built in Ireland.[29] This is equivalent to around 22 houses per thousand of the population. The equivalent number in Europe is around five houses per thousand of the population. After a slow start, the supply side of the industry reacted very aggressively. Arguably, the response was way too aggressive and too many houses were built all over the country, many of which are now lying idle. These houses may never be occupied because they were built in areas with no natural demand and very often on the basis of ill-advised tax breaks. These developments can be spotted on the way into most towns and villages in the country and will remain a blot on the landscape for years to come, unless a sensible decision is taken to knock them to the ground and return the land to agricultural use where it would be of more benefit to the country.

Whenever I reflect on this issue, I cannot help but think about an ugly tax-driven apartment block in a village in Waterford close to where I grew up. I will never comprehend how any local authority could ever have given planning permission for developments such as these. Different people have different views on this, with some believing that corruption created the basis for much dubious development around the country. There is certainly considerable reasoning behind such a claim, if the evidence presented at the various planning tribunals is anything to go by. It was also the case that local authorities encouraged development because it generated both once-off and ongoing revenues for local authorities, and boosted economic activity in an area. Unfortunately, things went totally out of control. These unfinished, empty buildings are set to become the tenements of the future.

Another big issue around the increased supply of housing over the past decade has to be the quality and suitability of that housing for future requirements in the context of an ageing population. On the quality issue, the paper-like walls in apartment blocks and non-detached houses have to be experienced to be believed. Furthermore, of the total house completions between 2002 and 2008, 26 per cent or 112,066 were apartments. Many are small one- or two-bedroom apartments, which will hardly be suitable for family requirements in the future. There has clearly been a distinct lack of foresight in our planning.

Net Result

The price of a house, like the price of most goods and services, is determined primarily by the forces of supply and demand, although market interventions influence outcomes in profound ways. Against a background of very strong demand and limited supply initially, house prices increased at breakneck speed in the period between 1995 and 2006. Early in 2007, the market started to lose momentum for no very obvious reason, other than a collective market realisation that prices had probably come too far and that the market had moved out of kilter with fundamentals. However, the tightening of ECB interest rates from 2 per cent in December 2005 to 4.25 per cent by July 2008 acted as a strong catalyst for the eventual turn in the market, as it showed non-believers that interest rates could go up as well as down. According to the Permanent TSB/ESRI house price index, national average house prices peaked in February 2007 and by August 2009 had fallen back by 24.4 per cent. The magnitude of this price decline is difficult to rationalise because most observant people would recognise that the value of housing has fallen back significantly in excess of 24.4 per cent. The problem is that market transactions died in 2008 and 2009 and, in a market where there are few transactions, it is difficult to price an asset. By the middle of 2009, house valuations had, according to my estimation, fallen back by around 45 per cent from their peak early in 2007. From peak to trough it is certainly possible that house prices could adjust by up to 60 per cent. There are some out there who believe that the correction could be even greater, such as Morgan Kelly in UCD. Who am I to disagree with him? After all, I thought he was way too pessimistic about the market back in 2007, but he has been proven right to date.

Before concluding this description of the development of the housing market over the past decade, I will leave the reader with one fact – back in 1995 the average new house price was 4.4 times greater than the average industrial wage and the average second-hand house price was 4.2 greater; by 2007, the average new house price was 10.3 times greater and the average second-hand price was 12 times greater.[30] Something was drastically wrong.

The message from the construction and housing experience of the past decade is that this was a situation that was allowed to get totally out of control. Through a combination of poor planning, irresponsible bank lending practices, investor greed, excessively low interest rates, and various incentives for house purchase and house building, the market was driven beyond what was fundamentally justified. House prices rose to amazing heights and the economy became totally dependent on and intoxicated by all things to do with housing. A serious economic and financial vulnerability was created, and has now been realised with devastating consequences. The key lesson to be learned is that nothing like this must ever be allowed to happen again.

That is easier said than done, however, and unfortunately history everywhere shows us that bubbles have a nasty habit of repeating themselves, largely due to human nature. Despite this inevitability, it is incumbent on Irish policy-makers to ensure that the madness of the past decade does not happen again. Much of what the economy is currently enduring is a result of regulatory failure. It is clear that the ability of financial institutions to extend credit must be regulated, and the types of innovative mortgage products introduced must be carefully controlled. As discussed in Chapter 7, the financial services industry is clearly not capable of regulating itself, so strong powers must be given to the Financial Regulator to do the job properly. The price of development land must also be controlled and local authorities should be forced to engage in better planning practices. Property tax incentives should also be phased out.

In the future a checklist must apply: LTVs in excess of 75 per cent must never be allowed; a mortgage should not exceed the old-fashioned salary requirements; no mortgage should be longer than 25 years; no development must be allowed without first providing infrastructure; there must be no tax reliefs; and local politicians should have no control over planning decisions.

When bubbles are allowed develop, they will inevitably implode with devastating consequences. It is hard to know when or what will cause the implosion. Hopefully, in the next cycle, increased regulation will make a bubble less likely.

5

Why Is Everything So Expensive in Ireland?
Cost Competitiveness and
the Spiralling Cost of Living

*Those people rushing up to the North to fill their car
boots with food and booze should put the savings made
into a deposit account to be eventually used to buy air-
line tickets to visit their children in Australia.*
Jim Power, November 2008

The Northern Pilgrimage

In the run-up to Christmas 2008, shoppers from all over the
Republic of Ireland were going up in their thousands to shop
in Northern Ireland. Long queues were commonplace from
the hill on the Dublin road right into Newry City and
beyond. This was a far cry from previous years when southern shoppers were going en masse to New York to do their
Christmas shopping, but during recessionary times people
have no choice but to slum it. During 2008 and indeed in 2009
it has not been uncommon to see southern registered cars
from as far away as Cork and Waterford in shopping-centre
car parks in places like Newry and Lisburn. This move north
to shop is not a new phenomenon and it did occur back in the
1980s, particularly in relation to electrical goods, which in
those days were considerably cheaper in the North. I bought
my first-ever radio cassette player in Jonesborough back in
the mid-1970s, for about half the southern price. However,

the shopping items today are different than in the past, with food and alcohol now being the favoured items.

A report[1] prepared by the Office of the Revenue Commissioners and the CSO published in February 2009 estimated that, in 2008, the value of cross-border shopping was in the range of €350 million to €550 million, up from between €210 million and €340 million in 2007. The resultant loss to the Irish Exchequer from these excursions north is estimated to be between €58 million and €90 million in VAT and excise duties, and between €15 million and €24 million in lost corporation tax receipts. This report did not factor in the tax implications of the job losses associated with the loss of retail activity in the South. Speaking at a Bord Bia food forum in Dublin in November 2008, I argued that those people who are travelling north to do their shopping should put the savings in a deposit account and build up the price of an air ticket to visit their emigrant children in Australia. This was not intended as a flippant comment, but one with the deadly serious message that, if Irish people continue to leave the jurisdiction to do their shopping, thousands of jobs will be lost.

It has been argued by some that this is an all-Ireland economy and that shopping in the North is not an issue. The reality of course is that it is not an all-Ireland economy. In fact, there are two very separate exchequers, and the increased tax revenues accruing to Her Majesty's Treasury from southern shopping expeditions does not find its way into the southern coffers. Nor will Her Majesty pay for the cost of the unemployment that will inevitably result from the outflow of retail spending from the southern economy. The aforementioned report prepared by the Office of the Revenue Commissioners and the CSO also predicted that, in 2009, there would be a further increase of between €100 million and €150 million spent in cross-border shopping, with further significant loss of tax revenues.

Notwithstanding arguments about economic patriotism, the main reason why shoppers throng north of the border to do their basic shopping is because many retail items are much cheaper in the North. Exchange rate movements also make it worthwhile to take the time and effort to travel north. Between September 2007 and the end of 2008, sterling declined by over 40 per cent against the euro. This immediately gave southern shoppers 40 per cent more purchasing power in the North, regardless of price differentials. The reality is that Ireland has become a very expensive country in which to live in recent years and the cost of living here is now one of the highest in the EU.

The Groceries Order

In a much heralded RTÉ television programme called *Rip-Off Republic* in August 2005, financial guru Eddie Hobbs highlighted the very high cost of living in the Republic of Ireland. The programme did not bring anything new or terribly revealing to the table but it did highlight what most people felt, namely that the cost of living in Ireland was incredibly high. At the time, this programme aroused a lot of angry comment and, more significantly, brought pressure to bear on the political firmament to address the issue.

The first and main casualty of this campaign by Hobbs was the Groceries Order. However, it has continued to reverberate through the Irish retail sector ever since, and the already mentioned sourcing move by Tesco in May 2009 was just another result of the price awareness that was created by Eddie Hobbs. The original Groceries Order was introduced in 1956 in order to abolish the practice of resale price maintenance. This practice occurred where suppliers set prices and kept them artificially high. The Order was amended in 1980 to ban below-cost advertising, and again in 1987 to ban below-invoice price selling and 'hello money'. The Groceries Order covered:

> grocery goods for human consumption (excluding fresh fruit, fresh vegetables, fresh and frozen meat, fresh fish and frozen fish which has undergone no processing other than freezing, with or without the addition of preservatives) and intoxicating liquors not for consumption on the premises and such

household necessaries (other than foodstuffs) as are ordinarily sold in grocery shops, and includes grocery goods designated as 'own label', 'generic' or other similar description.

In November 2005, not too long after Eddie Hobbs's intervention via the TV screen, the Minister for Enterprise, Trade and Employment Micheál Martin announced that he was going to abolish the Groceries Order, which duly happened in March 2006. It was abolished on the basis that it had kept the prices of the vast majority of grocery products in Ireland at artificially high levels by allowing suppliers to specify minimum prices below which products could not be sold.

When the Order was abolished, it was argued by many that it would result in significantly lower prices for the consumer. The evidence following the abolition of the Order shows that prices in general did not come down in any material way. In other words, the abolition of the Order did not result in the consumer bonanza that some were promising. This should not have come as a major surprise to any intelligent person, as the evidence backing up the assertion that the Groceries Order was contributing in a significant way to higher prices than would otherwise be the case was not very compelling. Arguably, the Order was good for competition and provided choice, value and convenience for shoppers, and allowed individual entrepreneurs to compete with the large multiples.

The bottom line in relation to the abolition of the Groceries Order was that Government was coming under increasing public pressure to address the cost of living in Ireland and it wanted to go into the 2007 general election arguing that it was proactively trying to reduce the cost of living for hard-pressed consumers. As is very often the case in Ireland's diluted form of democracy, many decisions are taken for reasons of political expediency rather than for real economic or social reasons. The abolition of the Groceries Order certainly fits the bill in that regard.

By focusing attention on the Groceries Order, the Government was able to deflect attention from the real drivers of inflation in the Irish economy.

The Real Drivers of the High Cost of Living in Ireland

Table 3 examines the price dynamics of a range of goods between 2000 and the middle of 2009.

Table 3: Selected Price Developments

January 2000–June 2009	% Change
Consumer Price Inflation	+33.3%
Food	+23.1%
Non-Alcoholic Beverages	+17.3%
Alcoholic Beverages (off-trade)	+19.8%
Clothing & Footwear	-26.8%
Water Supply & Refuse Charges	+257.5%
Electricity	+70.2%
Gas	+90.7%
Household Appliances	-13.2%
Health	+76.2%
Postal Services	+47.4%
Education	+78.6%
Health Insurance	+147.0%
Child Care	+84.8%

Source: CSO, *Consumer Price Index – Detailed Analysis*, June 2009.

In areas of the economy where there was intense competition both from within and outside the country, the change in price over the period considered was well behind that experienced in areas of the economy sheltered from competition and, in many cases, controlled by the state. In areas like health, education, local authority services, electricity and gas the rate of price increase has been well ahead of overall inflation in the economy. Many state suppliers of services have had to increase prices disproportionately in order to pay for the rampant growth in public sector pay, which was exacerbated by the first tranche of benchmarking in 2002.

At the time of the debate on the Groceries Order I believed and argued vehemently that food prices did not represent the big driver of inflation in Ireland, but they were of course an easier target than the monopolised and sheltered parts of the economy. I had no ideological hang-up about the Groceries Order, but it was diverting attention from the real issues. Interestingly, after the abolition of the Order, the Law of Unintended Consequences came into play. Off-licences and supermarkets engaged in aggressive price discounting of alcohol. Between March and December of 2006, the price of alcohol sold in the off-trade declined by 3.7 per cent, while food prices actually increased by just less than 1 per cent. In other words, the abolition of the Groceries Order had the effect of promoting the anti-social drinking behaviour that has become such a blight on Irish society, but it failed to result in significantly lower food prices. If this was what the proponents of the abolition of the Order were looking for, well then they were welcome to it.

The real issue of course is that, in recent years, Ireland has become an extremely expensive country to live in, to work in and to do business in. According to Eurostat,[2] Ireland was the second most expensive country in the EU in 2006, with the cost of living 25.4 per cent above the EU average. Back in 1998, prior to Ireland joining the single European currency, the cost of living in Ireland was 8.1 per cent higher than the EU average and there were six countries more expensive in the EU. This relative deterioration is due to the fact that, in the ten years since Ireland joined the EMU, inflation as measured by the EU Harmonised Index of Consumer Prices (HICP) has been higher in Ireland than in the Euro Zone as a whole in eight of the ten years. Average prices in Ireland increased by 39.2 per cent between 1999 and 2009, compared to a Euro Zone increase of 23.9 per cent.[3]

If prices in a country are increasing at a faster pace than in another country, there must come a point when the catch-up process is complete and that country becomes relatively more expensive. In Ireland's case, this is exactly what has happened over the past decade. The big question of course is why the inflation dynamics in Ireland have developed as they have.

There are many academic theories about how inflation is determined. I will not go into this in such detail, but I am going to identify some of the key factors that have driven Irish inflation to the point where people are compelled to queue to get over the border to Northern Ireland to fill the boots of their cars.

The price of anything is primarily determined by demand and supply, subject of course to external interventions such as regulation, taxation or exchange rates. Policy-makers can intervene in the price determination process through methods such as a ban on below-cost selling or through the imposition of taxation on a good or service, such as stamp duty on housing transactions or VAT on goods or services. For countries that import a lot of produce, the level of the exchange rate can have a significant impact on price. For example, if the euro falls in value against sterling, imports into Ireland, when converted into euro terms, will become more expensive.

For a small open economy like Ireland, with heavy external trade exposures, movements in exchange rates and price levels in countries from which Ireland is importing goods can have a significant bearing on inflation. Ireland is a textbook example of a small open economy with exports equivalent to 82 per cent of GDP and imports accounting for 71 per cent of GDP.[4] Prior to joining the EMU, Ireland's inflation was heavily determined by exchange rate movements, but this has changed significantly since then, given that around 30 per cent of imports in 2008 came from countries that share the same currency as Ireland. However, exchange rate movements against sterling and the dollar are still important because over 33 per cent of Ireland's imports originated from the UK in 2008 and almost 12 per cent from the US.

In considering Ireland's inflation performance since 1999, relative exchange rate movements have had some influence, but domestic factors have become increasingly important. As stated earlier, the general price level in an economy is primarily influenced by the interaction of demand and supply in the economy. Arguably, since Ireland joined the EMU in 1999, demand in the economy has been too strong, supply has not kept pace and prices have adjusted in an upward direction as a result.

The sharp divergence of Irish inflation from the EU average can be partly explained by the Balassa–Samuelson effect. This theory sounds complicated, but it is pretty straightforward. The theory argues that differences in the level of economic development and living standards across countries can lead to significant differences in non-traded prices. It postulates that high living standards are largely a reflection of high levels of productivity in the traded goods* sector of the economy, normally resulting in higher wages for those workers. The scope for productivity growth in the non-traded sector of the economy is much more limited, but wages will nevertheless be bid up in that sector, thereby leading to higher relative prices for non-traded goods. In Ireland in the second half of the 1990s there was a rapid catching-up process in terms of productivity and living standards, leading to costs in the non-traded sector rising more rapidly than in other countries, ultimately leading to higher relative inflation. Once the catching-up process is complete, real convergence should be achieved, but at a potentially high cost to the economy in terms of lost competitiveness, higher unemployment and lower growth. Ireland is now in the thick of this process, following a period of strong growth in wages and prices in the non-traded sector of the economy. We are now paying the price in terms of lost output and rising unemployment, as our international competitiveness has been seriously undermined.

One way of considering the demand and supply dynamic is to look at the concept of potential output and how it compares to actual output. Potential output is the maximum output that an economy can produce, given the capital, know-how and labour supply available. In other words, it is

---

*Traded goods are goods that can be traded between countries. Non-traded goods are goods that cannot be physically traded between countries. For example, housing is a non-traded good, while a car is a traded good.

the maximum output an economy can produce if all productive resources are being fully utilised. Potential output can of course increase by improving know-how in the economy through, for example, investment in education and training, inflows of new labour supply into an economy or investment in new capital equipment, particularly technology. Actual output, on the other hand, is what an economy actually produces. The difference between the two is what economists call the 'output gap'.

The rule of thumb is that, if actual output exceeds potential output, demand for products and labour tends to increase and prices and wages are bid up, or in other words inflation increases. On the other hand, if actual output is less than potential output, prices and wages tend to adjust in a downward direction, if left to do so. If, for example, a minimum wage exists in a country, there is a limit to how far wages can adjust in a downward direction. Another term to describe an economy where actual output is greater than potential output is an 'overheated' situation.

Between 1999 and 2006 economic growth in Ireland was exceptionally strong. Real GDP growth averaged almost 7 per cent per annum. House prices rose very strongly, as explained, and the economy effectively achieved a situation of full employment when the unemployment rate fell to a low of 4.2 per cent of the labour force early in 2005.[5]

In an environment of such strong demand, the prices of many goods and services were bid up, and workers were able to command higher wages because of the nature of the labour market. There is a vulgar joke about why dogs lick their private parts, the answer being that they do so because they can. The same analogy can be applied to the vendors of goods and services who increased their prices simply because they could in many cases. In relation to wages, the reality of the Irish labour market in the 1980s was that one was very lucky to get a job and did not have much bargaining power in terms of wage demands. This all changed utterly as we progressed through the 1990s and into the new millennium. Of course, in the face of higher wage demands, vendors increased prices to compensate for the higher wages and a classic old-fashioned wage–price spiral developed.

As well as general labour market conditions, the rapid escalation of house prices also fuelled strong wage demands. As house buyers were taking on bigger and bigger mortgages in the face of rapidly rising house prices, they sought higher wages to compensate and, as wages increased, this in turned allowed people to borrow more, thereby pushing up house prices further. The whole thing developed into a vicious price spiral and nobody shouted 'Stop!'

After we joined the EMU we lost control of interest rates and became subject to the interest rate policy laid down by the ECB in Frankfurt. Of course, in a monetary union, interest rates are set to suit the requirements of the bigger economies and the smaller economies just have to accept what they get. After the EMU commenced, the ECB set interest rates to satisfy the requirements of the big countries such as Germany, France and Italy. These rates were generally set at very low levels and arguably were way too low for the requirements of the rapidly growing Irish economy. In other words, low interest rates added fuel to a fire that was already burning very strongly. It doesn't take a genius to figure out that applying that much stimulus to an economy leads to overheating.

In a working paper[6] in 2008 the OECD concluded that, in Ireland between 1999 and 2007, inappropriately low interest rates resulted in a dramatic increase in house prices, a very strong increase in housing investment, a very strong increase in mortgage credit, a very strong increase in private sector credit and a moderate increase in stock market indices. Ireland was possibly the most overheated of all economies and the IMF stated that 'within the context of a monetary union, Irish fiscal policy needed to be substantially more aggressive than it was.'[7]

The Cost of Doing Business in Ireland

Much of the poorly informed discussion on the high cost of goods and services in Ireland fails to take adequate account of the cost of doing business in the country. At the end of the day, if the cost of doing business in an economy is high, then the vendors of goods and services will be forced to either cut margins as far as possible or increase the price of goods and services to stay in business. So, in understanding why the cost of living in Ireland is higher than in most of the EU, a range of business costs need to be examined.

There are a number of realities for Irish business relative to business in other EU countries. For most businesses, wages represent the single biggest cost. Between 1999 and 2007, average hourly earnings in Ireland increased by 65 per cent compared to an increase of 33.6 per cent in its major trading partners. Ireland also has the second highest minimum wage in the EU, which is currently €2 per hour higher than in the UK.

The *Annual Competitiveness Report 2008* from the National Competitiveness Council within Forfás highlighted some stark facts about the cost of doing business in Ireland. For example:

- The average rate of wage inflation between 2004 and the middle of 2008 was 50 per cent above the EU average
- Wage inflation grew by more than double the Euro Zone average in the construction and communications sectors between the middle of 2004 and the middle of 2008
- Industrial electricity prices are the second most expensive in the EU-15, largely due to a heavy reliance on imported fossil fuels. Household electricity prices were 28.7 per cent above the EU average in 2008 and were the second most expensive in the EU
- Industrial gas prices in 2008 were the fourth highest in the EU-27 and more than 25 per cent above the average. Household gas prices are 13 per cent above the EU-27 average.

The reality for Irish businesses is that most operating costs have gone up very significantly in recent years, including those relating to labour, fuel and electricity, property, waste disposal, security and transport. Furthermore, as an island nation, bringing the produce to market is generally much more expensive than in non-island nations.

Within the Euro Zone economic bloc, Ireland is unique in the sense that it has a much bigger trading exposure to countries outside of the Euro Zone than any other member country. For example, over 30 per cent of Irish imports are sourced in the UK. Around 42 per cent of imported consumption goods ready for use are sourced in the UK and, in the case of food, drink and tobacco, the UK accounts for over 55 per cent. It is therefore important to bear in mind that the UK is a significant source of consumer goods imports, and so exchange rate movements and transaction costs become a significant issue for the importers and the vendors of these products. Having said that, retailers importing from the UK have been very slow to pass on to the consumer the sharp fall in the value of sterling against the euro that has been occurring since September 2007. However, in the face of a serious loss of business to Northern Ireland, retailers have started to react, although it is not clear if these moves are in the best interests of the Irish economy in the long run. Many products that were previously sourced in Ireland are now being sourced in the UK, and Irish suppliers are being put under serious pressure to cut prices and pay for various price promotions. Undoubtedly, this will cost thousands of jobs in the Irish agri-food sector.

Ireland being an expensive country to live and work in is largely due to the fact that inflation has been allowed to run well ahead of that in the rest of the EU, since Ireland became a founding member of the single European currency. Inflation has been driven higher because policy-makers failed to pursue a fiscal policy that was consistent with the low level of interest rates set by the ECB and because of the weak exchange rate that prevailed in the early years of the currency experiment. Ireland joined the single currency at the peak of the economic cycle and was immediately exposed to very low interest rates and a depreciating exchange rate, both which served to exacerbate the boom. Policy-makers stood by and allowed this to happen. At the same time, the cost of doing business in the country was allowed to spiral out of control, but many people were so intoxicated by the whole environment that nobody objected in an effective way. Those who did were either pilloried or ignored.

If costs in an economy continually rise for a protracted period in excess of costs in the countries with which it trades, then the loss of competitiveness will eventually force an economic adjustment, which will normally involve lower growth and rising unemployment. Arguably, that is what has happened in Ireland in 2009. There is an upside to this adjustment process. As an economy moves deeper into recession, there is a good chance that the cost of living will start to adjust downwards. In the first nine months of 2009, inflation as measured by the HICP fell by 1.4 per cent, and by 3 per cent in the year to September 2009. The process must have further to go if Ireland is to adjust to the European cost of living.

It is essential that the cost of living adjusts further in a downward direction to restore price competitiveness in the economy. The challenge for policy-makers will then be to pursue policies that will ensure that price pressures do not intensify again. The traditional tools of economic management, interest rates and exchange rates are not available to the Irish authorities due to EMU membership, so it is essential that other tools such as a prudent fiscal policy and a restrained wage policy are used to control economic growth and hence inflation. In other words, the authorities will have to control the amount of fuel that they apply to the Irish economic fire. The key lesson to be learned is that, if economic growth is allowed to spiral out of control, inflation will take off as sure as night follows day.

6

A Litany of Policy Failures

Now everything's a little upside down, as a matter of
  fact the wheels have stopped,
What's good is bad, what's bad is good, you'll find out
  when you reach the top
You're on the bottom.

Bob Dylan, 'Idiot Wind', 1974

Irish policy-makers are currently struggling to grapple with many difficulties, the most serious of which are the effective insolvency of the banking system, spiralling unemployment, damaged competitiveness and an unsustainable public finance situation. Here, I'm going to take a look at how various policy failures such as wasteful public spending, flawed tax policies, social partnership and the inability to manage a small open economy in a monetary union all contributed to the problems that now necessitate a lot of painful medicine.

Taxation and Government Expenditure

Painful Medicine

It would certainly be possible to describe the Irish economy and its financial system as upside down and that the wheels have indeed stopped. The most painful reminder of how difficult things are in the economy in 2009 is provided by the *Report of the Special Group on Public Service Numbers and*

Expenditure Programmes published in July 2009. This group, affectionately known as 'An Bord Snip Nua', was set up by Minister for Finance Brian Lenihan in November 2008 to examine expenditure programmes in each government department and to make recommendations for reducing public service numbers in order to get the public finances back into a sustainable situation. The group was headed up by economist Colm McCarthy.

The fact is that, while the downturn in the international and Irish economy caused tax revenues to fall sharply and spending to increase as unemployment climbed, there is also a more fundamental structural problem with the public finances in Ireland. Basically, the base from which taxation is collected was allowed to narrow too much, while the base of spending was allowed to get too big during the period of the economic boom. The taxation issue is being addressed by the Commission on Taxation set up by the Minister for Finance.

In its report, An Bord Snip Nua goes through spending in every government department and raises questions about the necessity of provision of certain services, the reason why the public sector should be providing the services in the first place rather than the private sector, and the manner and efficiency involved in providing the services. As such, the two volumes of the report represent the best root and branch examination ever undertaken of how the public sector works and how taxpayers' monies are expended. In a time of scarce resources, this is a particularly valuable exercise, but one might naively believe that such analysis is done on an ongoing basis. That certainly does not appear to have been the case in Ireland.

The report outlines a menu of policy options for Government. The suggested savings as a result of this exercise is €5.3 billion and the suggested reduction in public sector staffing levels is 17,358. Three government departments – Education and Science, Health and Children, and Social and Family Affairs – accounted for 72 per cent of total monetary savings, and 75 per cent of total staff reductions. Unfortunately, these three areas are the most politically sensitive and brave or perhaps foolhardy political leadership would be required to deliver the suggested savings.

The key principle guiding the recommendations from An Bord Ship Nua is to basically introduce private sector work practices and efficiencies into the public sector. This is not to suggest that the private sector is always by definition efficient, and in fact it became clear during 2008 and 2009 that the banking sector in Ireland has been far from it in recent years. However, when inefficiencies exist in the private sector, they are generally identified and eradicated by market forces. This does not tend to happen in the public sector, which is typically sheltered from such forces.

The fact is that taxpayers' money is used to fund public services, so the taxpayer should feel entitled to a guarantee that the money is spent in the most efficient and effective manner possible. No vested interest group has the right to, or indeed should be allowed to, get in the way of achieving that objective. Unfortunately, under the social partnership model nurtured with loving care by Bertie Ahern, vested interest groups became too powerful and were allowed exert an inordinate influence on policy-making in general.

The cutbacks contained within the report from An Bord Snip Nua are pretty savage by any stretch of the imagination and will impose considerable pain on most segments of Irish society if implemented. However, it is necessary to restore some semblance of order to the public finances if eventual bankruptcy is to be avoided in the longer term. It is clear that if government expenditure had been controlled going back to 2000 and if Ahern's Governments had not acceded to the spending demands of every vested interest group, the recommendations contained in the report would not be necessary.

Taxation Policy

During the period of Bertie Ahern's leadership from 1997 to 2008, his two finance ministers, Charlie McCreevy and Brian Cowen, stood up in successive budgets and delivered the good news that more and more workers were being removed from the tax net altogether. Following Budget 2008, the Minister for Finance Brian Cowen informed us that 878,000 workers were then outside of the tax net completely, compared to just 380,000 when his Government took office in 1997.[1] From a social perspective, this represents great news because the fewer lower income workers paying tax the better. However, it is not economically sustainable. In addition to removing more and more workers from the tax net altogether, tax rates were reduced considerably. Over the period from 1997 to 2007, the standard rate of tax was reduced from 26 per cent to 20 per cent and the top rate of tax was reduced from 48 per cent to 41 per cent.[2] Over the same period a unified corporation tax rate of 12.5 per cent was introduced in order to satisfy EU objections about discriminatory tax treatment of different sectors. This represented an increase of 2.5 per cent for manufacturing companies, but a dramatic reduction in the tax rate for non-manufacturing activities.

In theory, this overall policy of reducing the tax burden was positive if one accepts the notion that lower taxation increases incentives and effort in society. I certainly do. Some people do not accept that notion and I have had several heated arguments with broadcaster Vincent Browne on his former RTÉ radio show and his current TV3 current affairs show. However, the experience in Ireland does support the notion that lower taxes are good for economic activity and employment, as it helps to encourage higher labour force participation and overall economic growth. For instance, the halving of the capital gains tax rate from 40 per cent to 20 per cent in Budget 2008 resulted in a sharp increase in revenues from this particular tax, as capital transactions increased dramatically in response to the lower rate. For example, in 1997 the total take from capital gains tax was €179 million; this had jumped to €880 million by 2001 and to €3.1 billion by 2006.[3]

The period from 1997 to 2008 did see a significant decline in the personal direct tax burden and the corporate tax burden. This helped to achieve greater economic efficiency, but unfortunately it was a flawed policy because it did not form part of a coherent plan for management of the public finances. For one thing, it is not possible to narrow the tax base indefinitely by taking more and more people out of the tax net as the successive Ahern Governments did. They did so on the basis that tax revenues would continue to flow from the property sector, but, as we now know, this was a dangerous assumption to make. Tax revenues from the property sector collapsed in 2008 and 2009, and the overall tax base was way too narrow to take up the slack; hence a huge hole has appeared in the public finances.

Government Expenditure

Of course, this policy of taking more and more people out of the tax net and reducing taxation might have been somewhat sustainable if spending was tightly controlled, but this did not happen. The attitude was that, if the money was available, it should be spent, regardless of how it was spent. Both Charlie McCreevy and Brian Cowen frequently repeated the mantra that public spending growth must be correlated with the growth in revenues. This was a very dangerous basis on which to manage the public finances. First, once committed to, public spending becomes embedded in the system, becomes a semi-permanent part of the cost base of the state and is extremely difficult to withdraw. This fact was clearly highlighted by the controversy that erupted following the decision in the Budget of October 2008 to take the medical card from many of the over-seventies. The same principle applies to government spending as to rearing children – once you give sweets to a child it is very difficult to take them away again without causing a major tantrum. The second problem with this policy of correlating spending growth with growth in tax revenues is that, if the base from which tax revenues are coming is transitory in nature, a vulnerability to a sharp slowdown in any area of the economy is created. As discussed in Chapter 4, the base from which much of Ireland's

111

tax revenues were generated in recent years was the property sector, and this dependency has been cruelly exposed over the past couple of years. Bertie Ahern's Governments appeared to spend money on the basis that property-related tax revenues would flow indefinitely. This was a big mistake.

Between 1997 and 2007, net voted current expenditure expanded at an annual average rate of 10.8 per cent, and between 2000 and 2007 the average growth rate was a massive 11.7 per cent per annum.[4] Such growth in spending on the day-to-day running of the country at the peak of the economic cycle, and Ireland was certainly at the peak of an economic cycle between 1997 and 2007, is criminal. It has created a serious crisis for the Irish public finances and efforts to claw back some of the committed spending are proving extremely difficult, to put it mildly. The incontrovertible fact that, while taxation is flexible in a downward direction, spending is not flexible in a downward direction was never grasped by Ahern's Governments and we are now paying the price.

Brian Cowen as minister for finance asked a number of interesting questions and made some interesting points in his Budget 2006 speech: 'It is not just a matter of the quantity of spending but the quality as well. Does it meet current needs and also provide for the future? Do we get full value for it? Could we achieve the same for less? These are issues which are rightly to the fore in the debate on public spending.' Similar rhetoric has been bandied about over the past decade, but it was empty rhetoric and nothing was ever really done to ensure that the issues raised by Cowen in December 2005 were tackled or indeed taken seriously. An answer to these questions was clearly provided in the report of An Bord Snip Nua in 2009.

The whole focus of Government was based on inputs rather than outputs. In other words, many government politicians have over the years continuously referred to the amount of money that was being spent in areas such as health and education, and indeed an awful lot of money was spent in these areas, but very little attention was paid to the outputs of this spending. The fact that An Bord Snip Nua's report had to rec-ommend expenditure savings of €5.3 billion is clear evidence of the wastage that has occurred and the excessive public sector cost base that has been allowed to develop over the past decade.

Fiscal policy describes the manner in which government spending and taxation are combined to influence economic variables in an economy. The sensible way to apply fiscal policy is on a counter-cyclical basis. This means that, when an economy is growing strongly, it is appropriate for gov-ernment to take money out through either tax increases or tight control of spending. The very opposite happened in Ireland over the period of Ahern's premiership; taxes were cut aggressively, and at the same time spending on the day-to-day running of the country was allowed to grow very strongly. This just pumped more and more money into an economy that was already growing very strongly and the result was the creation of a seriously overheated situation. This policy stance is described as 'pro-cyclical fiscal policy'.

Today, in the midst of a very deep recession, the Government is being forced to increase taxes and cut spend-ing, which is just serving to exacerbate the downturn in the economy. The appropriate thing to do in the midst of a reces-sion would be to cut taxes and/or increase spending. However, because of the sins of the past decade, such a policy stance is unfortunately not possible. It would not be inappropriate to describe Ahern's policy towards the econ-omy as displaying a high level of economic illiteracy.

The attitude that, if the Government has the money, it should spend it has resulted in serious wastage of valuable and scarce resources in the Irish economy over the past decade. This wastage occurred in many areas, of which the following are just a few examples, albeit very telling ones.

As discussed in Chapter 4, a huge amount of money was spent on incentivising building projects all over the country through various tax breaks. This helped create a massive building boom and saw the building of thousands of proper-ties around the country for which there was never going to be any natural demand. Many of these are now lying idle in an unfinished state.

Decentralisation is the second major money-wasting issue that comes to mind. In Budget 2002, Charlie McCreevy pulled the decentralisation rabbit out of the hat. On that day I was in an RTÉ TV studio analysing the Budget as it was being announced and my initial reaction to the plan to relocate thousands of workers and many agencies of government out of Dublin to the regions was positive. In the context of the Government's National Spatial Strategy, which was intended to deliver more balanced regional economic development, it appeared to make sense. However, by midnight on the night of that Budget I was beginning to doubt the sense of my initial reaction when I started to hear stories of populist politicians putting up signs in some constituencies claiming that they had delivered decentralisation. This smacked of political opportunism, but also sent out a worrying message that this was just a political ploy ahead of the 2002 general election. Later it became apparent that many of the decentralisation plans were not particularly consistent with the National Spatial Strategy and also that very little planning or thought had gone into this Budget-day announcement. From the taxpayer's perspective, the real crux is that the Government has spent millions of euro buying up sites around the country to house the decentralised agencies, most of which will not now be used. Many of the sites were bought close to or at the peak of the property price bubble and today are worth considerably less than what was paid for them. For example, over €10 million was spent on two sites in County Waterford, both of which are lying derelict and probably will be for quite some time. Decentralisation has now been suspended pending a review in 2011, but not before it cost the taxpayer an awful lot of money.

The famous e-voting machines also rank well up there in terms of wasting taxpayers' money. Initially, I naively believed that this represented a good idea as it was furthering Ireland's claim to be a 'knowledge economy'. However, the expensive machines turned out not to be fit for purpose and were subsequently put into storage at great cost to the taxpayer, not to mention the €50 million or more that was spent on them in the first place.

The expansion of the public service during the boom is another cost that the Government must contend with today. The employment breakdown in Table 2 (see Chapter 4) also shows the extent to which employment in the public sector expanded. In the period 2002 to 2007, employment in the public sector expanded by 94,500 and accounted for 27.6 per cent of the total jobs created in the economy over the period.[5] This is despite the fact that in Budget 2003 the Minister for Finance Charlie McCreevy stated that 'the Government has decided that numbers employed across all sectors of the public service are to be capped at their present authorised levels with immediate effect. In addition, the Government has decided that there will be a reduction of 5,000 in those numbers over the next three years.'[6] At that point there were 360,000 employed in the public sector. In the second quarter of 2009 there were 485,900 people employed, representing an increase of over 120,000.[7] So much for a restraint on employment in the public sector!

Public sector pay also expanded strongly over the period. For example, between 2002 and 2007 average weekly earnings for workers in the civil service increased by 33.8 per cent, while earnings in the public sector (excluding health) increased by 31 per cent.[8] In Budget 2003, Minister McCreevy had also pledged restraint in relation to the level of pay increases in the public sector. This was not delivered and, due to this combination of strong growth in numbers employed and earnings, the public sector pay bill got out of hand.

There are many other examples of money wastage, including the failure to monitor spending at FÁS, the PPARS health service computer system, the huge cost overruns on major infrastructure projects such as the Dublin Port Tunnel, the various tribunals that have made multimillionaires out of many legal eagles at the expense of the taxpayer, and the vast amount of money that has been and continues to be spent on renting school prefabs. The list just goes on and on, but time and space unfortunately limit my ability to keep going. The clear message is that, over the past decade, vast amounts of money were spent on a range of projects and activities, many of which were directed towards dampening dissent from various vested interest groups. The money could and should have been used more prudently, because it is unlikely that the Irish economy will ever again be capable of generating resources of the magnitude generated between 1997 and 2007.

One of the more interesting and very revealing aspects of 'Bertinomics' was the grand vision Bertie had of building a national stadium that would commemorate his period as taoiseach. Bertie's pet project, affectionately known as the 'Bertie Bowl', smacked of the tendency of Eastern European communist leaders to build expensive monuments as permanent legacies of their leadership. The estimated cost of the development rose to more than €1 billion, yet he remained hell-bent on seeing it through. However, in the aftermath of his crushing victory in the 2002 general election, Ahern's Government was forced to engage in some spending cutbacks in the face of more challenging economic times as a result of the bursting of the dot-com bubble in the US. In the face of cutbacks in many areas of social spending, it was inconceivable that the project could go ahead, and Michael McDowell's intervention was instrumental in finally burying the notion. The only element of the project that went ahead was the National Aquatic Centre, at a cost of €70 million to the taxpayer. This pool later leaked, had part of the room blown off and eventually had to be taken over by the state. The incredible thing is that Bertie Ahern wanted to expend that much money on a stadium in a country that had and still has inadequate provision of basic services such as health care, education and child care. Amazing stuff!

As the economy lies mired in deep recession in 2009, and as the public finances continue to deteriorate, it is clear that there was an abject failure to achieve a sustainable public finance situation in recent years and the whole public finance edifice was clearly built on foundations of sand. This crisis in the structure of the public finances must rank as one of the key legacies of Bertie Ahern's period in charge of Ireland. The practical implication of this failure is that the Government is now being forced to take money out of the economy in the midst of the deepest recession in modern Irish history. That is not the way an economy should be managed.

Social Partnership

When Bertie Ahern stepped down as taoiseach in May 2008, his successor Brian Cowen wrote that 'as Minister for Labour he was instrumental in putting in place the social partnership model for national agreements, and today it continues to play a significant role in underpinning the sustainable development of our economy.'[9] This assessment is accurate to a certain point. Putting social partnership in place back in 1987–88 was good for the Irish economy. It provided wage stability and brought industrial peace to Ireland after years of serious unrest and excessive wage growth. Putting in place a structure that delivered such stability was good for employers because they could plan with certainty, and it was particularly good for multinational companies operating here or wanting to operate here. It was beneficial for workers because it brought a significant reduction in the personal tax burden as well as a much more buoyant economy with more employment opportunities. It was also very good for the trade union movement as it gave them renewed influence at a time when unions representing private sector workers were waning in influence. As we progressed through the 1990s the social partnership model gradually expanded to bring many diverse interest groups into the process, with the Social Pillar becoming increasingly influential. A nice cosy club developed and over the years we were treated to TV footage of the various social partners making their way into Government Buildings with a smug look on their faces that said, 'We are members of this cosy club which gives us unbridled access to the corridors of power ... we like it and we are getting fat on it.'

I believe that, in its first decade or so, the social partnership model worked well for Ireland by bringing a sense of policy stability that had been absent for a long time, and the process created an economic and social framework for the country. However, it eventually outlived its usefulness and, once Ireland moved into an environment of virtual full employment in the late 1990s, social partnership ceased to be effective.

Trying to put an artificial constraint on wage growth in an environment of full employment simply does not work. In the labour market environment in which Ireland found itself by the late 1990s and thereafter, employers were forced to pay higher and higher wages to recruit and retain workers and, despite the existence of a theoretical cap on wage growth, wages started to rise quite strongly across many sectors of the economy. In 1999, I presented a paper at the annual Dublin Economics Workshop in Kenmare arguing that the whole process should be either changed to adjust to different economic labour market circumstances or else be given a Christian burial. On the following Monday I got a call from a senior body in Bank of Ireland to drop up to the bank's head office in Baggot Street in Dublin to explain my heretical views. It was pointed out to me in no uncertain terms that it was not appropriate to be so critical of Government policy and also that social partnership wage restraints actually suited the pursuit of massive profits within the bank. It is ironic in hindsight that the financial institutions were so preoccupied with staying on the right side of Government, given what we now know about the mess they were building up for the country.

While the labour market was adjusting to the full-employment situation and wages across many sectors were steadily increasing, Government delivered on its side of the bargain and continued to cut taxes and committed to serious growth in public expenditure. Quangos and various other committees were set up to deal with every conceivable issue. The legacy of social partnership is that there are now thirty Oireachtas committees operating at great expense to the taxpayer.

In overall terms, Government more than delivered on its side of the social partnership bargain, but it did not get wage stability in return. Under the social partnership model, many of the various spending programmes and quangos identified in the report from An Bord Snip Nua actually thrived and prospered.

There also has to be a serious question mark over the democratic nature of the whole social partnership process. The various social partners, including the trade unions – particularly the public sector unions – the employers' group IBEC and the Social Pillar, which includes bodies like the Conference of Religious in Ireland (CORI), have exerted an enormous influence over the manner in which the Irish economy and Irish society have developed over the past couple of decades. These bodies and the individuals representing them are not elected by the people of the nation. The electorate votes for politicians to run the country and take the hard decisions that are needed, with the back-up and support of the permanent administration. Instead, the political system has abdicated responsibility to the non-elected social partners. Personally, I have never been terribly comfortable with the notion of people such as Father Seán Healy of CORI, Turlough O'Sullivan, the former head of IBEC, and trade unionists such as David Begg and Jack O'Connor being instrumental in shaping the policy decisions that govern my everyday life and that of my children.

We should also never forget that social partnership gave us the fiasco of benchmarking. In 2000, under the terms of one of the social partnership agreements, the *Programme for Prosperity and Fairness* (PPF), the Government and the social partners entered into a commitment to find an appropriate way of benchmarking public sector pay to pay in the private sector. The objective of the exercise was to try and ensure that the public sector would be in a position to recruit and retain the staff necessary to deliver the quantum and quality of services that the public was entitled to expect. The process involved an evaluation of public sector pay and jobs by reference to their equivalents in the private sector.

Prior to benchmarking, public sector pay had been determined in a very unsatisfactory manner. While the pay of a small number of pivotal grades in the public sector had been determined through comparison with the private sector, pay rates for a large number of other grades had been determined by a complex system of internal and cross-sectoral relativities. This resulted in situations where one segment of public sector workers might strive for and achieve better pay and conditions, and this would then set in train a process where other public sector workers in similar grades would seek a similar settlement, and other grades would then seek to maintain their pre-existing relativities. This typically resulted in a situation where a cycle of leapfrogging claims developed, and a poor industrial relations climate was the order of the day. This was clearly unsatisfactory and had to be changed. Hence the benchmarking process was born.

Under the terms of the PPF, the Public Sector Benchmarking Body (PSBB) was set up. Between May and October 2001, 3,994 public sector workers participated in a detailed job evaluation exercise with the co-operation and assistance of their trade unions, associations and employers. Between October 2001 and February 2002, a further 3,563 jobs in the private sector were evaluated, again with the help and co-operation of a number of representative bodies and a large number of private sector companies. The PSBB also received a number of submissions from interested parties and got advice and assistance from expert professional consultants (if that is not an oxymoron) and international agencies.

The terms of reference or driving principles in the whole process were as follows:

- A quantitative and qualitative evaluation and measurement of work
- Comparisons with the private sector
- The elements of reward in the public and private sector
- The incompatibility of cross-sectoral relativities and the need for internal consistency and coherence
- An examination of personnel issues in the public service, such as recruitment and retention
- The need for equity between public sector and private sector employees

- The impact of pay on national competitiveness
- The overriding need for modernisation and change in the public sector
- The value of public sector pensions relative to those in the private sector
- An examination of other material sectoral differences in conditions and benefits, such as security of tenure and benefit in kind.

On the surface it appeared that the benchmarking process had solid justification in an economy of full employment where the public sector seemed to be struggling to compete with the private sector for employees. However, subsequent developments strongly suggest that a major opportunity was missed to engineer reform in the way that public services are delivered.

The PSBB issued its final report in June 2002, *The Report of the Public Service Benchmarking Body*. It made two recommendations. First, it suggested a number of changes to public service personnel management practices, or, in other words, a modernisation process for the public sector. Second, it suggested a range of pay increases linked to agreements on modernisation and change. This was the 'ATM machine' that Senator Joe O'Toole had famously referred to in anticipation of the benchmarking process.

The recommendations on modernising work practices in the public sector date back to the Strategic Management Initiative (SMI), which was launched in 1994. This initiative set out three objectives: to make a greater contribution to national development, provide excellent service to the public and make the most effective use of resources. This initiative was expanded and developed over the following decade with the publication of *Delivering Better Government* in 1996 followed by a further set of objectives under the terms of the PPF in 2000, which pledged to introduce new performance management systems, integrated human resource management strategies, improved organisational flexibility, better training and development, and stronger organisational capability. In the *Sustaining Progress* social partnership agreement in 2004 further commitments were made, aimed at achieving maximum value from all public spending.

The jury is out on whether these objectives have been even partly achieved, but there is certainly evidence in some parts of the public sector of improved efficiency and customer service. The Revenue Commissioners have certainly developed their use of technology and now make it very easy to pay tax and claim entitlements, and the online motor taxation process is incredibly efficient and customer friendly. I have dealt with the Central Statistics Office for over twenty years and in that timeframe the level of customer service has improved dramatically, and technology has been embraced in spectacular fashion. However, there are many other areas of the public sector where the quality of service is very questionable. The Health Service Executive (HSE) immediately springs to mind.

The benchmarking report recommended variable pay increases across many sectors. The increases varied from a 2 per cent increase for laboratory technicians to a 25 per cent increase for various ambulance grades, and a wide range of increases in between. The overall average increase in public sector wages was 8.9 per cent. This benchmarking increase was in addition to agreed increases under the national wage agreements and was backdated to December 2001. It was indeed a bonanza for most public sector workers and, somewhat surprisingly, all of the social partners went along with the recommendations because they were not willing to rock the social partnership boat. As well as increasing wages for existing workers, benchmarking also impacted positively on public sector pensions. Indeed, one retired economics lecturer told me of his surprise when he received a cheque for his backdated benchmarking award, which he regarded as quite bizarre, not to mention disturbing. I estimate that, by 2008, benchmarking had added close to €2 billion per annum to the public sector pay and pensions bill.

Amazingly, IBEC went along with the charade, which I believe should be to that organisation's eternal discredit. I made myself incredibly popular with IBEC when, following the implementation of benchmarking, I suggested in an RTÉ

TV interview with George Lee that any self-respecting member of that organisation should resign from it. Perhaps this was a tad harsh, but I for one will never understand how an organisation purporting to represent employers' interests could ever have signed up to such an agreement. On the other hand, to their eternal credit, the public sector unions delivered in exemplary fashion for their members. Whether it was in the national interest or not was only of secondary importance.

The first benchmarking process turned out to be seriously expensive and added considerably to the annual cost of running the state. It lacked any semblance of transparency because we never discovered the rationale for granting the various awards. It pushed up the cost of public services and thus contributed hugely to the cost of living and to the loss of competitiveness in the economy. And, after all this, it is not clear that it did much to improve the delivery of public services across many parts of the public sector. The non-implementation of any real performance measurement was a mistake and a missed opportunity. For example, all teachers got the same award, regardless of how good, bad or indifferent each individual teacher was. This must have been very demoralising for the very good teachers who gave more than 100 per cent to the job.

The second benchmarking body reported in December 2007 and, in recognition of very changed economic circumstances, it granted pay increases totalling just €50 million, equivalent to an increase of just 0.3 per cent in public sector payroll costs. It was a bit more upfront about its deliberations and stated, for example, that the superior public sector pension arrangements should be quantified as 12 per cent of salary and that this should be taken into account when comparing remuneration levels in the public service and private sector. In any event, the public sector unions were not happy with the overall conclusions and felt their members were entitled to another ATM bonanza.

In the very changed circumstances that the Irish economy now finds itself in, thousands of private sector workers are losing their jobs and many of those who are lucky enough to be still in jobs are facing significant reductions in wages. Yet the public sector unions are not prepared to contemplate any wage cuts amongst their members, despite the fact that CSO data suggests that public sector average hourly earnings were 47.6 per cent higher than the private sector in October 2007. Granted, 52.8 per cent of public sector workers had third-level qualifications, compared to 31.9 per cent in the private sector. Consequently, you would expect public sector workers to earn higher salaries. However, even adjusting for this differential in educational attainment, public sector wages are still about 20 per cent higher than in the private sector. In a 2009 report, the ESRI estimated that between 2003 and 2006 the public sector pay premium increased from 14 per cent to 26 per cent.[10]

In an environment where private sector wages are lower than public sector wages and where private sector wages are falling, the logic of benchmarking would appear to suggest that public sector wages should be adjusting in a downward direction. However, the stance of public sector unions indicates that benchmarking is a process that is adjustable in one direction only. The clearest indictment of the whole benchmarking process is that An Bord Snip Nua's report recommends many of the measures that benchmarking was meant to address in the first place.

Bertie Ahern has got great credit for keeping social partnership alive, but this is not appropriate or deserving. In my view, social partnership did nothing to prevent the current economic crisis from occurring, and in fact contributed hugely to it: cost competitiveness has been seriously eroded; the quality of public services – with a few exceptions – has generally not improved very much; Ireland's infrastructure is still lacking in first-world quality; the construction sector became the only sector that mattered in the economy at the expense of many other more productive sectors; the public sector unions were allowed become way too powerful; and Government spending was let spiral out of control. Social partnership should have been given a Christian burial a decade ago.

Ireland in the EMU

Ireland became a founding member of the EMU upon its inception on 1 January 1999. Ireland qualified because it easily satisfied the Maastricht convergence criteria. I believed and argued vehemently in the 1990s that it would not be in Ireland's best interests to participate in the process from the beginning, and indeed Britain's non-participation gave us a good escape clause. In October 2000, I testified at the invitation of Sir Norman Lamont before a UK House of Lords sub-committee on Ireland's early experience within the EMU. I was not very positive about the early experience, much to the annoyance of my politically correct Bank of Ireland employers at the time.

My scepticism about Ireland's participation in the great monetary experiment was based on two premises. First, Ireland would be the only country in the single currency with a greater trade exposure to countries outside the regime than within it. Since the small and medium enterprise (SME) sector still has an inordinate dependence on the UK market, this would inevitably prove very difficult for that sector of the Irish economy from time to time. We are currently in one of those periods, with sterling trading at 92 pence against the euro, which is causing serious difficulties for the SME sector. Second, I did not believe and still do not believe that the Irish political system is capable of managing an economy in a monetary union. This belief was based on my observations of how the economy was managed within the old ERM. I believe I have been totally vindicated.

In the EMU Ireland lost control of its currency and its ability to control interest rates. This left the country with two main tools of independent economic management: fiscal policy and wage policy. The reality in the EMU is that the European Central Bank (ECB) sets interest rates to attain its primary objective of keeping inflation close to 2 per cent. This means that the ECB will always set interest rates based on economic conditions in the big European economies such as Germany, France and Italy. What happens in Ireland will have no bearing whatsoever on the interest rates set by the

ECB. In other words, Ireland is a price taker rather than a price maker in terms of setting interest rates. If interest rates as set by the ECB actually suited Ireland, this would be no more than a coincidence. The policy implication of this is that a country like Ireland should use its fiscal policy and wage policy in a manner that is consistent with interest rates as set by the ECB and the level of the euro as determined by the foreign exchange markets. This has not happened.

Ireland became a member of the EMU close to the peak of the Celtic Tiger and immediately inherited a very low level of interest rates and a very weak euro, both of which gave a significant boost to an economy that was already growing very strongly. In this environment, the Irish Government should have been tightening fiscal policy and keeping a lid on wage growth in order to counteract the very low level of interest rates and the weak currency. As explained earlier, neither of these two things happened. Fiscal policy was very loose with tax cuts, strong spending increases, and serious tax incentives for the property and construction sector. Wages also grew very strongly in a fully employed economy, thanks to the inappropriate social partnership policy. The net result was that an already very strong Irish economy was blown into the stratosphere.

Due to the Government's failure to manage the Irish economy in a prudent way in an EMU environment, the ability to cope with asymmetric shocks was seriously impeded. We are now living through that reality. Some commentators such as Eddie Hobbs and David McWilliams have suggested that Ireland should leave the single currency, re-establish the pound and restore competitiveness by allowing the new independent Irish currency to fall sharply in value. Such a suggestion does not make sense at this juncture. If Ireland were to leave the single currency arrangement now, already fragile international confidence in the economy and its financial markets would be destroyed and the country could become another Iceland within six hours. Ireland is where it is and it is now imperative that policy decisions are made that will help restore competitiveness and make life in the single currency regime somewhat more comfortable. Leaving the system from a position of such weakness would not be advisable.

Bertie Ahern was taoiseach during most of the first decade of Ireland's membership of the EMU and it is clear from the manner in which he and his two finance ministers managed the economy that they had no understanding or perhaps willingness to accept the disciplines inherent in such a currency arrangement. Ireland is now paying the price for this mismanagement and it could take years to get the economy back on an even keel. Hopefully lessons have been learned which will inform our future leaders.

The Ahern Legacy

As the old joke goes, a recession is when your neighbour loses his job and a depression is when you lose yours. This black humour is resonating with many Irish people at the moment as job losses mount in all sectors of the economy, including the professional classes, which would generally be regarded as fairly immune to economic downturn. Even economists are losing their jobs in the current recession, which really does feel like a depression to me.

In the world of economics, a recession is defined as two successive quarters of negative growth in economic activity. Ireland satisfied this criterion in 2008. A depression is generally defined as a contraction of 10 per cent in economic output from peak to trough. Ireland unfortunately meets that criterion as well and it is certainly conceivable that the contraction from peak to trough could come close to 15 per cent. The Economist Intelligence Unit (EIU) stated that the extent of downside risk to the Irish economy appears to be 'without precedent' By the time the global recession ends, Ireland will have the dubious distinction of being the advanced economy to suffer the largest contraction in economic activity during this period of global turmoil. This is all pretty grim stuff, but much of it could have been avoided.

In its 2009 staff report on Ireland, the IMF stated that Ireland was particularly vulnerable to the recent global shocks 'given its serious internal imbalances'. It cited over-extension in construction and financial intermediation along with a loss of international competitiveness as the key imbalances in the economy. In other words, if regulation of the banking system had been properly applied, if planning policy had been more sensible, if tax breaks for development had been much less generous, if Government had controlled public spending in a prudent manner and if Government had fully understood how a small open economy in a monetary union should be managed, we would not be in the position we are in today. Our current situation could also have been avoided if the Irish in general had not lost the run of themselves and got caught up in an irrational spending and borrowing binge of unprecedented proportions. There was nothing Irish policy-makers could have done to prevent the subprime-induced global economic recession, but if the economy had been more prudently managed during times of plenty, the ability to cope with and respond to the external shock could have been seriously enhanced.

As applied in Ireland between 1997 and 2008, 'Bertinomics' basically entailed a total failure to control public expenditure, giving the public sector trade unions whatever they desired in order to keep the social partnership process together, and generally following populist economic policies. Bertie Ahern was an incredibly skilful politician and was adept at smothering political dissent. He presided over a period of rapidly rising salaries for politicians and created a myriad of Oireachtas committees that all combined to keep political dissent to a minimum. He lacked any long-term strategic economic vision and appeared to believe that, as long as the developers were pumping out housing, and generating lots of jobs and tax revenues in the process, everything was hunky dory.

The economic ideology that succeeded Bertinomics is called 'Cowenomics', which basically revolves around trying to clean up the mess created by Bertinomics. It is still too early to make any definitive judgments on Cowenomics because Bertie Ahern's successor has been flapping about trying to pick up the pieces after a decade of economic mismanagement. The mess is quite a big one and the sense of anger amongst the Irish populace is palpable.

The really depressing thing is that, after a decade of such strong growth and revenue generation by the state, the general quality of public services is still well below what one would expect in a first-world developed economy. A major opportunity has been missed and it is difficult to see how lost ground can be reclaimed in much more difficult economic times. Oh Bertie, it could have and should have been so much better!

7

Conditions for Recovery

*History teaches us that men and nations behave wisely
once they have exhausted all other alternatives.*

Abba Eban

Hope in Every Crisis

In the midst of an unprecedented economic crisis it is hard to
see where economic recovery could possibly come from and
there is a strong temptation to plunge into the depths of
despair, but that is not in the nature of the human spirit.
There are still many individuals and companies operating in
the Irish economy who believe in the future of the country
and who will continue to try to make it happen. The challenge for policy-makers is to create an environment where
such individuals and companies are facilitated to the greatest
extent possible in order to create economic activity and
employment, and help Ireland realise its economic potential
once again. Recovery is possible, and we have the 1980s to
remind us of that.

In the 1980s there was also little belief in the ability of the
political firmament to extricate the economy from the mess it
was in. As mentioned, it was through a combination of luck,
sensible policy-making and, most importantly, strong political leadership that the economy managed to lift itself out of
its diffcult situation.

For Ireland to emerge from the current deep malaise, a
number of things need to happen: the global economic cycle

has to improve; the crisis in the banking sector needs to be sorted out to get credit flowing in the economy again; the economy should become more competitive; the structure of the public finance system must be re-engineered to make it more sustainable in the longer term and better able to cope with future shocks; the damaged reputation of Ireland has to be repaired; and an economic plan needs to be put in place, identifying the sectors that can contribute to Ireland's economic future. The global economic situation is obviously outside of Ireland's control, but the others are well within our own remit and must be tackled as a matter of urgent priority. This chapter examines the difficulties currently facing the global economy and, as well as examining prospects for global economic recovery, it identifies the conditions necessary for an Irish economic recovery.

Global Economic Turmoil and Subprime Madness

It is a historical fact that recessions that are caused by a shock to the financial system tend to be deeper and more difficult to emerge from than shocks to some other part of the economic system. For example, the recession induced by the bursting of the dot-com bubble in 2001 proved quite shallow and did not last very long. This is because it centred on a specific part of the IT industry in the US. While it did cause the US economy to go into recession and the global economy to slow markedly, it did not spread far outside the confines of the IT industry and equity markets.

There was a strong official response to the dot-com-induced slowdown. Interest rates were cut almost everywhere and fiscal policy was loosened. The global economy responded very quickly and a deeper recession was averted. The global financial system was not too adversely affected. It is worthy of note that the US economy was saved from a deeper recession by the continued ascent of house prices through the dot-com-induced recession against a background of historically low interest rates. This kept the

US consumer alive because a lot more personal wealth in the US is tied up in housing rather than in equity markets. However, ultimately the low level of interest rates and the strong growth in house prices sowed the seeds for the sub-prime debacle that has pushed the global economy into the deepest recession since the 1930s.

The evolution of the subprime bubble in the US is quite a complicated story, but it can be condensed without losing too much. As the Chinese economy emerged over the past decade, there were huge flows of capital into the US financial system, probably more than it could cope with. Faced with this massive inflow of liquidity and tighter banking margins as a result of intense competition in the US banking system, US banks identified subprime lending as a profitable busi-ness opportunity. They targeted potential customers who, for a variety of reasons, were high-risk from a credit per-spective and, as such, found it difficult to access normal lines of credit. These high-risk borrowers were persuaded to buy property and take out mortgages, initially on favourable terms, but after a period of time they were obliged to pay interest rates at least a couple of percentage points above normal borrowers. These high interest rates were very prof-itable for the lending banks and they did not perceive much risk in such lending activities. After all, US house prices had been rising for a decade and this was expected to continue. So, even if the high-risk borrowers defaulted, the banks always had the security of the property upon which the mortgage was granted. The lending banks became so excited by such profitable lending that they decided to take tranches of these mortgages and create investment products which offered high rates of return. These investments were then sold on to other banks, hedge funds, private investors and pension funds all around the world. The proceeds from the sale of these mortgage-based investment products were then used to extend further subprime mortgages. This whole process was facilitated by the development of innovative financial market products like 'credit default swaps' and

Collateralized Debt Obligations (CDOs), which nobody really understood but which the global financial system bought into.

Through this process, the risks inherent in the subprime mortgage market were spread around the global financial system. Regional savings banks in Germany and credit unions in Ireland, and thousands of other institutions besides, suddenly found themselves exposed to a phenomenon that they or most others couldn't possibly understand. Basically, an old-fashioned pyramid scheme was created and, amidst the euphoria, a frightening exposure was built up by the global economy and financial system to a seriously risky lending activity. Eventually, and not surprisingly, the original borrowers started to default and house prices started to collapse, particularly those of sub-standard properties that provided security for subprime lending.

From spring 2007 the whole house of cards started to teeter in dramatic fashion. Venerable US banking institutions such as Lehman Brothers and Bear Stearns collapsed and the whole global financial system was plunged into a crisis that was considerably worse than the Great Depression. I was in San Francisco on Saint Patrick's Day 2008 when Bear Stearns collapsed. The shock that the collapse of the fourth biggest investment bank in the US created in the US was quite immense and convinced me that we really had no conception on this side of the Atlantic of what was about to go down. I came back to Ireland and my subsequent commentary and analysis of the Irish economy became distinctly more downbeat, although I now realise in hindsight that it was not downbeat enough.

I also remember doing an investment seminar in Nenagh in April 2008 with an investment adviser from Ulster Bank, which is part of the Royal Bank of Scotland Group. She boasted of the fact that the Royal Bank of Scotland had a higher credit rating than AIB or Bank of Ireland and that it was a much safer bet than the Irish banks. She was right about the status of AIB and Bank of Ireland, but when I got back into my car I was amused to hear on the 11 O'Clock

News that Royal Bank of Scotland had announced a record fundraising initiative to help it cope with serious damage to its capital base. Very few banks escaped the effects of one of the biggest financial disasters ever to befall the global economy and nobody could afford to be arrogant or smug, or cast aspersions on other financial institutions.

The net result of this whole subprime debacle is that serious damage has been done to the global financial system and credit availability has become a huge issue for the global economy. Regardless of what we think of banks and bankers, and having worked for 20 years of my life in banking I don't think a lot of a number of them that I came across, a properly functioning banking system is essential for an economy to work. Banking is a simple business, involving taking money from people who want to save and acting as an intermediary for passing the money on to people who want to borrow. Unfortunately, it is a simple business that was seriously complicated by people who believed they had become the masters of the universe. Bankers moved from being facilitators of wealth creation and economic activity to a situation where they believed they had become the actual creators of wealth and economic activity. It was a lesson on keeping a proper perspective on your role in life and not believing your own spin.

We know about the economic fallout from the collapse of the subprime mortgage market and associated investment products. For example, the US economy recorded a decline of 5.4 per cent in GDP in the final quarter of 2008 and 6.4 per cent in the first quarter of 2009.[1] Europe and the UK have fared little better. That is a dramatic decline in economic activity by any stretch of the imagination. In response to this situation, interest rates in the US, the UK, Japan and Europe have been taken down to exceptionally low levels, several countries introduced significant fiscal stimulus packages, with President Obama leading the way, and massive amounts of money have been injected into banking systems around the world. In other words, global authorities are throwing the kitchen sink at the unprecedented difficulties.

This will eventually work and, in fact, by the middle of 2009 there were clear signs emerging that the downward momentum in the global economy had been arrested. It remains to be seen what the recovery process might be like, but, given the massive destruction of personal wealth, the huge fiscal deficits that have been created and the damage done to the global financial structure, it would come as a surprise to me if the global economic cycle were to rebound strongly. It is more likely to be a slow and gradual path to recovery.

One positive impact of the implosion of the US subprime market was that it stopped the developing Irish subprime mortgage market in its tracks. Not surprisingly, some institutions in Ireland were starting to warm to the notion of lending money to high-credit-risk individuals. Based on the track record of the Financial Regulator in regulating the banking system, it was unlikely that much would have been done to prevent this practice from emerging. Indeed, over the past couple of years the subprime lenders, or the 'specialist' mortgage lenders as they prefer to call themselves, have been appearing quite a bit in the commercial courts as they move in on borrowers who should never have been allowed anywhere near a mortgage in the first place. Subprime lending is an evil, because the reality is that there are some people in society who simply should not be given access to credit. Thankfully, Ireland has been spared the problems relating to subprime lending; our mortgage market already has enough difficulties.

The Irish Banking Crisis and NAMA

It was quite astounding to hear the former Chairman of AIB Bank Dermot Gleeson, at the MacGill Summer School of 2009, blaming all and sundry for the mess Ireland is now in, including economists and amateur landlords, and almost everybody else in the country. Mind you, he graciously, but somewhat grudgingly, accepted that his own bank was not entirely blameless in the whole sorry affair. Surely he must realise that the cavalier attitude that bankers showed towards lending and risk assessment in recent years and the failure of the Regulator to regulate the banks are where the key faults lie. Of course, there has got to be some element of personal responsibility but, when offered money by banks, the majority of people cannot help themselves. Unfortunately, the current and future generation of taxpayers will end up paying for the folly of the banking industry. No wonder many people are so annoyed, and comments such as those by Dermot Gleeson will not alleviate that anger. Our current generation of bankers should be made to wear sackcloth and ashes for the foreseeable future and own up to some of their misdeeds.

The Irish banking system has been at the eye of a serious storm since the beginning of 2008, but the problems were already mounting in 2007. The basic problem in the Irish banking system was the fact that many bankers lost the run of things and created utterly ridiculous and unsustainable exposures, particularly to developers. It is astonishing to discover that, for example, the top 50 customers of AIB owe the bank €19 billion and account for almost 15 per cent of all lending by that bank.[2] The group of companies controlled by developer Liam Carroll owed €1.1 billion, while a recent court case revealed that a relatively unknown developer in Cork, John Fleming, owes more than €1 billion to the banks. It is absolutely astounding that the banking system could have allowed such irresponsibility. The Irish banking crisis of 2009 will undoubtedly feature in future books on economic and financial mania and madness.

I recently heard one retired bank chief executive, whose portfolio of 'blue chip' bank shares was decimated, ruefully lament the fact that the banking industry had torn up the rules of lending. As well as tearing up the rules of lending, they lost all understanding of the concept of risk and how to measure it. This was not helped by the presence of one bank in the system that really tore up the rules of banking – Anglo Irish Bank. It is often the case in banking crises that one or two particularly aggressive banks push the boat out and the other banks are forced to follow suit. If they refuse, they can lose market share and the share price could in turn under-perform. This would then expose the management to criticism from the media and from shareholders demanding shareholder value. Anglo Irish Bank was an incredibly aggressive player in the banking market and forced the other banks to follow suit. As far back as the late 1990s, I attended meetings of the Court of Directors of Bank of Ireland where Anglo's activities in the market would often be discussed. Anglo Irish Bank clearly had no understanding of concepts such as risk and economic cycles and bought totally into its own PR spin. I approached Anglo Irish Bank for a job in the early 2000s and, after a number of meetings with various senior bodies, I was told by the then Head of Treasury Tiernan O'Mahony, who later went on to great fame with International Securities Trading Corp (ISTC), that I was a luxury the bank could not afford. That was probably a polite way of telling me that I was not up to the job. Whatever the reason, I still thank God every night for my lucky escape.

The public is utterly confused about the real status of the Irish banking system at this stage and one gets a strong sense that the Government is also pretty confused. The various banks claimed up until quite recently that all was well and that they did not need an injection of capital from the state. Then they admitted to their difficulties and started accepting capital, following a realisation that they could not possibly raise sufficient capital in the marketplace. The state was forced to guarantee the deposits and other liabilities of the Irish banking system at the end of September 2008 and then to nationalise Anglo Irish Bank in January 2009. In the Supplementary Budget of April 2009, the Minister for Finance Brian Lenihan announced the setting up of the National Asset Management Agency (NAMA) to try to sort out the crisis in the banking system.

NAMA is being set up on a statutory basis under the aegis of the National Treasury Management Agency (NTMA), which is the statutory body that manages Ireland's national debt. The plan is to transfer assets, primarily land and development loans, to NAMA. The aim of this is to remove the toxic assets from the balance sheets of the banks so that they be put in a position where they can start lending money again. In practical terms this means that NAMA will buy loans with a book value of approximately €77 billion at a price of around €54 billion from the banks. In reality, the loans are probably worth at most 40 per cent of book value, given the collapse in land and property prices, but if such a low price was paid the capital position of the banks would not be improved and lending could not resume. The higher price being paid means that the Irish taxpayer will be footing an inordinately large bill. However, the Irish Government and the taxpayer appear to be left with little choice if the banking system is to resume its role in the economy. NAMA does not represent a bailout of developers; it is quite simply a bailout of bankers.

The transfer will add to the gross national debt of Ireland, but in theory this will be offset by the assets taken in. However, with the assets being bought at a price above their market value, they will not offset the price paid. The idea is that the agency will then work to get the loans paid back in the normal way, but, given the amazing exposure that the banks have to developers, it is inconceivable that taxpayers' money will be fully recouped. Furthermore, the process of working through the loans and disposing of land and properties could take a decade.

The bottom line is that there is no easy solution to this crisis and there is no painless way out of it. It would be tempting to suggest that the banks be left to sink or swim and the state set up a new bank and start from scratch, using the money to be paid by NAMA to buy the assets as capital for the new bank. However, it is not clear to me that this would work because a collapse of the existing banking system would do untold damage to the Irish economy and the international reputation of Ireland. There is also the small matter of the deposit guarantee scheme in place since September 2008. Mind you, knowing what we now know about the activities that went on at Anglo Irish Bank, that particular institution should have been allowed to collapse in

September 2008. It would be no loss whatsoever to the Irish economic and financial system.

There is still considerable disagreement amongst experts on banking about the best way to handle the banking situation. Some argue that the banks should be nationalised to limit the taxpayers' exposure, while others believe that the NAMA solution is the only way out. Whatever option is chosen, we can be very certain of two things. First, it will be a very slow and painful process of recovery for the Irish economy and taxpayer and, second, if Ireland is to have any chance of emerging from the current morass anytime soon, a properly functioning banking system will have to be engineered as quickly as possible.

The Competitiveness Imperative

During the period of strong post-Celtic Tiger growth in the Irish economy, when consumer spending and house building assumed a preeminent role in driving growth, NCB Stockbrokers[3] argued that strong growth in population and labour supply would maintain a capacity for growth in Ireland that would far outstrip that in other EU countries where the demographic outlook is far less favourable. The suggestion was that Ireland's demographic profile was such that the growth in domestic demand would be sufficient to drive the economy forward and that exports would not be as important. The problem with this argument is that growth in the labour supply would just result in higher unemployment and/or emigration, unless the proper structures to support growth are in place. In my view, the key requirement for a small open economy like Ireland is to have a strong export base on which to support growth in the labour force and domestic demand.

The challenge for Ireland over the next couple of years is to ensure that, as the international economic cycle gradually improves, the Irish economy will be in a position to exploit that recovery. Key to this is the requirement to be competitive.

In any discussion on competitiveness, cost is normally the issue that tends to dominate. While cost is an important aspect of competitiveness, it is not the only issue to be considered. There are also non-cost elements that must be taken into account. As discussed in Chapter 5, on the cost front, it is an incontrovertible fact that Ireland has become a lot less competitive in recent years. This loss of competitiveness is amply demonstrated by the hoards of people travelling to the North of Ireland to stock up on consumer goods, those who travel to Romania to have their dental work carried out and, of course, those companies that are moving jobs out of Ireland to cheaper locations. In January 2009, Dell announced that it would move all production of computer systems for customers in Europe, the Middle East and Africa from its plant in Limerick to its Polish facilities and third-party manufacturing partners over the following year. This resulted in a cut in its workforce in Limerick by 1,900. In July 2009, Intel in Leixlip announced that it was cutting 300 jobs in that plant. The *Irish Times* reported that Intel signalled to staff that its manufacturing plants in Arizona and Israel were ahead of Ireland in terms of 'competitiveness and requirements on costs, skills and capacity.'[4] These are just two examples, but it is clear that Ireland's declining competitiveness has become a major issue for an economy operating in a difficult global market where competition from low-cost countries is becoming increasingly intense.

The Central Bank of Ireland measures Ireland's competitiveness compared to its international trading partners based on exchange rate movements and relative inflation. This Harmonised Competitiveness Indicator (HCI) shows that, in nominal terms, Ireland's external competitiveness deteriorated by almost 25 per cent between January 2002 and June 2009, reflecting an appreciation in the value of the euro, which tends to make Ireland's exports more expensive. When adjusted for inflation differentials, the real deterioration in competitiveness was 27 per cent. The basic interpretation of these numbers is that Ireland has become a lot less competitive relative to the countries with which it trades. This is not good for economic growth prospects.

The competitiveness imperative is quite simple and there are some encouraging developments. Private sector wages are adjusting in a downward direction in most industries, with the exception of banking, and the cost of living is falling. However, there is still a lot of progress to be made across the broader economy. The country needs to re-establish its export credentials and cannot go back to an economic model based on building houses for each other, selling cars to each other, and buying goods and services from each other, unless there is strong growth in productivity. Domestic demand has got be built on a solid export base, and trade unions and all other stakeholders need to get real about the mess Ireland is in; if competitiveness is not restored then Ireland will not share in the probable global economic upturn over the next couple of years.

If Ireland were a company experiencing the sort of trading difficulties that the country is currently grappling with, the policy options would not be difficult to figure out. These would revolve around cutting costs, controlling spending, and improving efficiency and productivity. Growth must be backed up by productivity and not debt.

On the cost front, private and public sector wages need to fall (that is already happening in the private sector), fuel and energy costs must come down, commercial rents must fall, professional fees such as medical, dental, legal, accounting and IT must adjust to the new reality, local authority charges and commercial rates need to fall, and lower house prices must be allowed evolve.

Productivity is defined as output per worker, and improvements in productivity represent the only way to generate meaningful economic growth and prosperity. So, on the non-cost front, areas such as IT capability, the quality of the IT offering, education and training, management skills, the quality of physical infrastructure, marketing skills, production skills and innovation all need to be improved for higher productivity.

On the IT front, Ireland is still scoring very poorly in terms of broadband penetration and quality following the flawed decision to hand over the national telecommunications company and infrastructure to a series of venture capitalists. These venture capitalists have been much more interested in extracting as much money as possible out of the business, and have not invested in the capital infrastructure necessary to deliver high quality broadband.

Creating Sustainable Public Finances

According to the projections contained in the Supplementary Budget presented in April 2009, the Exchequer is expected to collect €35 billion in revenues and to engage in net current spending of €46 billion, giving a current account deficit of €11 billion. It expects to run a deficit of €9 billion on the capital side of the budget, giving an overall Exchequer borrowing requirement of €20 billion. When this is adjusted to take into account the financial activities of local authorities and semi-state bodies, the general government deficit (GGD), which is the EU measure used to assess borrowing, is projected at €18.4 billion, equivalent to 10.75 per cent of GDP. The maximum borrowing permitted under the terms of the EU Stability and Growth Pact is 3 per cent of GDP, which would equate to €5.1 billion. At the end of September 2009, the Minister for Finance admitted that the tax take will be another €2 billion lower than expected and that the GGD will be in the region of 12 per cent of GDP in 2009. The numbers demonstrate clearly the crisis in the Irish public finances that cannot be allowed go unchecked for very long.

The key problem for the Irish public finances is structural in nature. The base from which taxes are collected narrowed too much during Bertie Ahern's reign, and, as mentioned, became very heavily dependent on the property and construction sectors. On the expenditure side, the spending base was allowed to grow too rapidly and, as explained earlier, once committed to, spending becomes more or less embedded in the permanent cost base of the country and is very difficult to row back on from a political perspective.

In the Budget presented in October 2008 and the Supplementary Budget of April 2009, the bias in government policy has been towards increasing personal taxes to bridge the gap between spending and taxation. The *Report of the Special Group on Public Service Numbers and Expenditure Programmes* identified potential expenditure savings of €5.3 billion. Cutting spending by this magnitude would be very difficult and would cause considerable pain to many sectors of Irish society. However, there would not appear to be too many options. The report highlights very clearly many areas of wasteful spending and inefficiencies in the public sector. These must be addressed because increasing the personal tax burden any further in an environment where consumers are under serious pressure could seriously undermine economic activity further and this would become self-defeating.

The base of spending has to be brought down, but reform of the tax system also has to be part of the solution. The big spending areas such as health, education and social welfare must be seriously examined in order to ensure that wasteful spending and fraud are cut out. The key emphasis in relation to spending must be on the quality of spending rather than the quantity. Quality really means getting value for money from every euro spent and ensuring that the spending is necessary and not wasteful. The base from which taxation is collected also has to be broadened and designed in a manner that would make tax revenues less dependent on the economic cycle. A property tax should be designed to replace the existing stamp duty property tax, which is based on the number of transactions in the housing market. Some form of carbon tax will have to be introduced and possibly a country-wide water tax. Creating as much certainty as possible in tax receipts is essential. The most economically efficient tax system would be one where there is a wide base and low marginal rates.

Creating a more sustainable fiscal situation is essential for the future prosperity of the economy. In the past decade, the economic and budgetary forecasting record of the Department of Finance has been poor, and this has given rise to significant overshooting of tax revenues, which resulted in a situation where the need to control spending did not appear to be very compelling. In 1997, the incoming Minister for Finance set a target of keeping growth in nominal net current spending to an annual average growth rate of 4 per cent over the life of the Government. This target or indeed subsequent efforts to control spending were not successful to put it mildly, and major growth in the spending base occurred. This cannot be allowed to continue because, in an environment of slower economic growth in the medium term, tax revenues are likely to grow much more slowly than over the past decade, and the ageing of the population will create longer-term pressures on public spending. Greater transparency and accountability will be required in the future to ensure that the public finances remain in a stable state and that expenditure is put to productive use.

Restoring Ireland's Reputation and Regulation

Reputation is extremely important for a small open economy like Ireland, which is dependent on foreign direct investment by overseas companies, and for investment in Irish financial markets. Up until 2007, Ireland had attained a strong reputation. Unfortunately, much of the international coverage of the Irish economy and its financial system has been very negative over the recent past. We should not fool ourselves that the foreign investment community is permanently thinking about us. However, it is a fact that any time the Irish economy or banking system has featured on the international radar over the past couple of years, it has been for all the wrong reasons. The collapse in the economy and the public finances certainly sent out a very negative message about Ireland, as did the collapse in the Irish equity market and the requirement for the Government to bail out the banking system. Many countries have had their own share of difficulties but these problems were undoubtedly worse in Ireland than elsewhere. However, the revelations about corporate governance issues in relation to Anglo Irish Bank, Irish Life and Permanent, and the Irish Nationwide Building Society were the straws that broke the camel's back. Incompetence is one thing, but the revelations from those institutions is a different matter entirely and a much more serious one. The failure of the Regulator to control the excesses in the banking system and, more importantly, the failure to identify the wrongdoings in these financial institutions do not send out a very positive message about Ireland as a place in which to do business. Big countries and big economies can possibly get away with such improprieties, but for Ireland is a much more serious matter.

A friend of mine who works in the Irish funds industry spends a lot of his working life overseas trying to attract overseas business. Over the past year, the first half hour of every meeting is taken up with effort to dispel notions that Ireland is a basket-case economy with a seriously flawed and dishonest financial system. Unfortunately, a few rogue bankers have done untold damage to the reputation of Ireland and it is now incumbent on our policy-makers to try to rectify this situation.

The regulatory regime needs to be strengthened considerably. I once naively believed that self-regulation or a principles-based approach to regulation would be most appropriate in order to make the environment as flexible and business-friendly as possible. I was clearly as wrong as I could possibly be. Self-regulation does not work in the Irish system, nor does a principles-based approach. A rules-based approach that is rigidly applied is now essential to try to convince investors that Ireland is a good place in which to do business.

Banking must now be tightly regulated to ensure that prudent loan-to-value ratios are adhered to, that exposure to individual sectors of the economy is limited and controlled, and that bankers start to behave as merely facilitators of wealth creation and economic activity. The remuneration structures in banking also need to be controlled, because incentivising bankers on the basis of the quantity rather than the quality of the products they sell is a recipe for irresponsible behaviour and, ultimately, disaster. The Financial

Regulator will have to be given real teeth and have the necessary personnel to use those teeth.

Regulation is also an issue in relation to the construction sector. The notion of quality versus quality must become the guiding principle. Ireland now has enough offices, industrial and retail developments, and apartments. It is time to cease building until the excess supply is eradicated from the system. The future of construction activity must be geared towards quality and satisfying real requirements in areas such as roads, hospitals and schools.

Unfortunately, the majority of bankers and developers have shown a total inability to behave sensibly and they have, and can in the future, get carried away by the greed factor. Given this reality, there would appear to be little option other than to ensure that regulation is strong enough to help and control those who clearly cannot help or control themselves.

One of the very practical but costly implications of Ireland's loss of reputation is the increased interest rate that the Government has to pay to foreign investors who are prepared to invest in Government debt. Given that the Government will be forced to borrow billions for the foreseeable future, this is a very costly loss of reputation. It is one thing making a mistake or being incompetent in one's job, but it a different matter entirely to engage in practices that fly in the face of probity and good corporate governance. Those people who engaged in such activities will have to be taken to account and never again be allowed to play any part in Irish corporate life. If a business or a country loses its reputation, then it has nothing. We should always remember that.

8

Developing a Plan

You can always amend a big plan, but you can never expand a little one. I don't believe in little plans. I believe in plans big enough to meet a situation which we can't possibly foresee now.

Harry S. Truman

We Must Have a Plan!

One thing to note about the last decade of Irish economic and financial history is that there would appear to have been very little in the way of strategic planning or thought guiding the evolution of the economy. The attitude towards the management of the public finances was cavalier. Once the money was around it was spent, and the tax base was decimated by ideological blindness and short-term thinking, not to mention political populism. Furthermore, successive governments were prepared to ride the construction boom for all it was worth and grow the public sector as if it were the highest value-added sector in the economy. There was no real attempt made to develop other sectors of the economy to ensure that we had a diversified and sustainable economic model. Clearly, a different approach is now required.

In the run-up to Ireland's membership of the EMU, I got involved in many spats with politicians and policy-makers over Ireland's suitability for the EMU. In my view it has been conclusively proven that the management of the Irish economy over the past decade was deeply flawed and failed to take any cognizance of the disciplines required for a small open economy in a monetary union. Irish policy-making has succeeded in creating a seriously uncompetitive economy, with many structural problems that have been cruelly exposed by the collapse of the housing bubble. History is useless if we learn nothing from it.

Creating a sustainable fiscal situation is obviously of crucial importance, but a strategic and long-term approach to the structure of the economy is also vital. One of the key principles of sensible investment is to manage risk through diversification, or, in other words, not to put all the eggs in one basket. Recent Irish Governments allowed most of our economic eggs to be put into the construction basket and, intoxicated as they became by the economic and financial riches thrown off by the construction sector, they neglected to ensure that there was a sustainable parallel economy operating and developing alongside the construction economy. As the economy became inordinately dependent on the construction sector, policies were directed towards growing that industry. Unfortunately, this was to a large extent at the expense of other sectors of the economy. Many businesses simply could not compete with the bloated construction industry for capital and labour and an unbalanced economy was created. Policy-makers failed to create a fallback position once the construction sector inevitably ran out of steam.

Such an inordinate dependence on a single sector must never be allowed to happen again. I believe that it is now incumbent on Ireland's policy-makers to plan for a more diversified economic offering. This strategy has to revolve around identifying a number of economic sectors in which Ireland can actually compete and ensuring that, insofar as possible, an environment is created whereby those sectors can develop. The economic plan for Ireland will have to combine the modern with the traditional, the old with the new, and the indigenous with the foreign-owned. It is not a case of either/or, but rather some of both.

Foreign Direct Investment

The foreign-owned multinational component of the economy has got to remain an important part of the model. The Industrial Development Authority (IDA) is the state agency with responsibility for attracting foreign direct investment into the Irish economy, and it has achieved considerable success over the past three decades. Part of its mission statement makes it very clear what the objective is – 'We will win for Ireland, its people and its regions the best in international innovation and investment so as to contribute to the continued transformation of Ireland to a world-leading society which is rich in creativity, learning and personal and social well-being.'[1] According to the IDA's *Annual Report* for 2008, IDA-supported companies employed over 136,000 people in permanent employment in 2008, exports from these companies totalled €92 billion, total payroll costs amounted to €6.7 billion, they paid €3 billion in corporation tax in 2007 and contributed €16 billion in direct expenditure to the Irish economy. Despite the popular perception, the multinational sector is still a significant contributor to the Irish economy and its continued prosperity is important. Having a strong foreign-owned component in the economy is good for the external image of Ireland; it ensures that modern techniques and work practices are continuously introduced to the Irish workplace, and, very importantly, it generates lots of indirect employment.

The ability to attract new foreign direct investment into the Irish economy and holding on to what we already have is becoming more challenging. The 12.5 per cent corporation tax rate is a necessary, but no longer sufficient, condition for Ireland's continued success in the foreign direct investment arena. Many emerging economies, particularly in Central and Eastern Europe, have replicated or improved upon Ireland's model for attracting foreign direct investment, and they are able to offer a much lower general cost base than Ireland. When launching the IDA's *Annual Report* for 2008 in July 2009, the IDA's chief executive warned that, in a small number of IDA client companies, Irish workers were earning

15 per cent more than their counterparts in sister companies in the US, and that wage levels were threatening Ireland's competitiveness. These comments elicited a very negative reaction from the trade union movement, but this is just indicative of the failure of the trade union movement to acknowledge that it has had any role to play in Ireland's economic difficulties. These are the very people who will be out in the media moaning about job losses in multinational companies, though they are apparently not prepared to countenance any level of flexibility.

As mentioned in Chapter 7, to remain a player in the foreign direct investment arena, the following will have to be addressed: the quality and accessibility of infrastructure, the level of broadband penetration and our cost competitiveness across the board. Most importantly of all, Ireland must continue to supply a highly trained and educated workforce. These are the minimum conditions necessary to ensure a continued strong contribution by the multinational sector to the Irish economy.

Agri-Food Industry

I have always lamented the fact that mainstream economists rarely, if ever, mention the agri-food industry when analysing the Irish economy. It is as if it is regarded as a poor relation of the 'star' sectors of the past decade, particularly construction and financial services.

Given that the construction and financial services industries are not likely to be leading the Irish economic charge for quite some time, we will be increasingly forced to depend on sectors that actually make something useful to drive future prosperity. In my view, the agri-food industry is one such sector. It includes everything from farming to food manufacturing and much more in between. I have a vested interest of sorts in the agri-food industry as I was brought up on a farm in County Waterford and have always passionately believed that it is an industry that is undervalued by policy-makers. However, it makes a huge contribution to rural economic activity and, more importantly, can make an even greater contribution in the future.

The facts in relation to the industry are pretty impressive:[2]

- Some 230,000 people are directly employed in the Irish food and drink industry
- For every job in food manufacturing, there are four related jobs in the wider economy
- The food and drink sector buys 80 per cent of its raw materials and services in the Irish economy – valued at €8 billion in 2007
- The value of goods and services (gross value added) for the food and drink industry was €27 billion in 2007, with an embedded Irish economy value of €22 billion
- On average, 80 per cent of production in the food and drink sector is exported, valued at more than €8 billion in 2007
- Given the very low import content, food and drink exports account for 20 per cent of Irish economy net export values.

Put simply, the agri-food industry is a major employer in the Irish economy. It sources much of its raw material domestically, it is dominated by indigenous companies and, very importantly, it plays a key role in the economic and social life of regional and rural economies. Despite the strong economic contribution, the industry is very often the victim of ill-informed commentary and policy-making. This was particularly true during the debate on the Groceries Order. Ireland must not be pushed in the direction of cheap food at any cost because the economic, social and health implications would be very negative. The cheap food policy pursued in the UK in the 1980s made a significant contribution to the BSE crisis, because food producers were basically forced to cut corners and sacrifice quality and safety to remain viable in the face of falling prices. If the Irish continue to push for cheap food, then quality will inevitably suffer. Given the importance of food to health, this would be a shortsighted approach. It has amazed me that, in recent years, one can buy a chicken at a lower price than a litre of beer. There has to be something wrong with that state of affairs.

The key to unlocking the obvious potential of the Irish food industry is through new products, quality and strong brands. Without new products, Ireland will be condemned to be a simple producer of commodities. The number of jobs we can create from producing and selling commodities is limited and, with increasing automation, it is shrinking rather than growing. The success of products like Baileys Irish Cream and the other brands it has inspired clearly shows what a new product backed by a strong brand can do. Indeed, the success achieved by Flahavan's in County Waterford provides a very strong template for what can be achieved in the sector. The basic product at Flahavan's is porridge manufactured from locally produced oats, but the company has developed the basic product into a number of innovative variations, such as flapjacks and a microwave single-helping breakfast product, to name but a few.

It appears to me that the Irish food industry is now under serious threat. Adverse currency movements, a high domestic cost base and increased overseas competition are all putting serious pressure on the industry. However, recent developments at retail level pose an even greater threat. In May 2009, retail giant Tesco moved to source more of its groceries from the UK to replace products previously sourced in Ireland, all in the name of delivering a cheaper product to the consumer. In June 2009 I suggested to the Oireachtas Joint Committee on Agriculture, Fisheries and Food that this move by Tesco could mark the first step in turning the Irish retail food and drinks market into an offshore version of Inverness. Irish consumers would be left with less choice and, more worryingly, the very survival of Irish food and drink producers could be seriously threatened. If Irish brands are locked out of a major retailer in Ireland and if other retailers are forced to follow suit due to competitive pressures, their ability to survive, let alone launch new products, would be severely threatened. Without a home market, Irish food companies will not have a market on which to launch and test new products before targeting export markets. This could seriously threaten thousands of jobs in the Irish agri-food industry.

In September 2009 I agreed to chair a new initiative by the Irish food and drink industry, called 'Love Irish Food'. This initiative has involved a number of Irish food and drinks companies – ranging from very large producers such as Glanbia to small artisan producers – coming together in order to create a new brand or logo that will signify that certain products are Irish in the true sense of the word. The criteria for displaying this new logo are that at least 80 per cent of the product must be made in the Republic of Ireland and, where possible, the manufacturer must use ingredients sourced in the Republic of Ireland. The key aim of this initiative is to inform consumers about which brands are Irish and which are not. This will help consumer choice and it is hoped that it will spark a change in consumer thinking by making people aware of the positive consequences for the economy of buying Irish food and drink brands.

Government needs to get serious about the farming and food sector and allow it to realise its undoubted potential as a high value-added component of the Irish economy. The decision to abolish the Rural Environment Protection Scheme (REPS) in farming, and the suggestion from the *Report of the Special Group on Public Service Numbers and Expenditure Programmes* that schemes such as the Suckler Cow Scheme should be terminated would represent more nails in the coffin of Irish farming and the Irish food industry. The Suckler Cow Scheme was introduced to improve the quality of animals from the suckler herd and thus improve the quality of Irish beef. Does its proposed abolition suggest that producing quality beef is no longer a priority? Likewise, the REPS was introduced to improve the quality of the rural environment and thereby improve the rural tourism product as well as aiding farmers. Does its abolition suggest that these issues are also no longer important? If so, this represents very short-term thinking.

Farming and the food industry have got to be nurtured and developed, because they offer significant growth potential for the overall economy. It is also important from a social and economic point of view that rural areas are not totally denuded of people and economic activity. The official attitude towards farming and the food industry is not consistent with the objective of the National Spatial Strategy launched in 2002, which is to 'deliver more balanced social, economic and physical development between regions'. This has not worked to date, and the current deep recession will now just serve to exacerbate the regional divergences in economic performance.

There is no reason why Ireland cannot become the Silicon Valley of food production, given its natural advantages as a food producer and the green image of Ireland. An artisan food industry, such as the thriving one in France, is capable of being developed in Ireland, provided of course that the red tape and bureaucracy are reduced. The over-application of health and safety regulations in Ireland makes it difficult, if not impossible, for small local producers to sell produce at local markets. In France, such small markets happen in every village around the country and, as well as supporting the local producers, they make an enormous contribution to the French tourism brand. Why can this not happen in Ireland?

Tourism

The tourism industry in Ireland is diverse. It includes everything from city breaks to river cruising, walking and cycling, and much more besides. It is another slightly 'old-fashioned industry' that was somewhat forgotten and perhaps taken for granted during the boom times, as 'sexier' areas flourished. As is the case with the agri-food sector, the growth potential of tourism will now have to be explored and exploited to the greatest extent possible. Like the agri-food sector, it is also an indigenous industry with a high labour content and it buys most of its raw material domestically. In 2008, 7.4 million overseas tourists visited Ireland.

Expenditure by those tourists was estimated at €4.8 billion. Another €1.5 billion was spent by domestic tourists.[3] The industry is now under pressure due to the global recession, the weakness of the dollar and the high cost of the Irish tourism product. In the first quarter of 2009, the number of overseas visitors to Ireland was 9 per cent down on the previous year.

There is nothing that the Irish tourism industry can do to influence the value of the dollar or global economic activity, but it can and must improve the competitiveness of the product. The cost of living in Ireland must be addressed and the quality of the tourism product must be improved. For policymakers, investment in the tourism product makes economic sense because, without ongoing upgrading and investment, the quality of the product will just deteriorate and the decline of the industry will be inevitable. Although it may not be regarded as a sexy industry by the economic elite, it is a high value-added indigenous industry that is of vital importance to rural and regional economies around the country.

Alternative and Renewable Energy

The cost of energy in Ireland was identified by the National Competitiveness Council as a major contributor to the high cost of living and the high cost of doing business in Ireland. As mentioned in Chapter 5, Ireland is the second most expensive country in the EU-15 for industrial electricity and is close to 40 per cent above the EU average. This situation is due to 'a heavy reliance on imported fossil fuels, exposure to global fuel price increases, low levels of spare generation capacity, poor availability performance and the relatively small scale of Irish generation plants and limited competition in generation and supply.'[4] There is a strong possibility – although nobody can be really sure given the doubts about peak oil – that, as the global economic cycle gradually improves over the next couple of years, the price of oil could rise rapidly again. In terms of future planning, the safest assumption to make is that oil and gas prices will be considerably higher in the future than they have been in the past. Working on the basis of that assumption, which is something that economists are very good at doing, it is imperative for Irish policy-makers to ensure that alternative energy sources are explored and delivered.

I remember, as a teenager in the 1970s, the protests and the concerts at Carnsore Point in County Wexford over the proposal to build a nuclear power plant there. It is still not very politically correct in the Ireland of today to explore or discuss the nuclear option, but yet we are more than happy to import electricity into Ireland that is generated using nuclear power. We will have to put aside our hang-ups and prejudices and seriously consider the possibility of building a nuclear power plant in Ireland.

Alternative energy, such as wind, solar, wood and marine biomass energy, are all possibilities. I am not an energy expert, but it is clear to me that Ireland has to develop alternative sources of energy. If we don't, we will remain an economic hostage to the oil and gas industry, and energy costs will remain an ongoing source of serious competitive disadvantage for Ireland.

Thankfully, there are enterprising and creative souls out there in Irish society who are giving this issue a lot more thought than our strategically deficient policy-makers. In the summer of 2009, an initiative was launched by a group of dynamic, enterprising and strategic thinkers called Spirit of Ireland. The basic aim of this initiative is to create a massive source of electricity based on wind energy. The West of Ireland seaboard is among the most exposed to wind in Europe, but it is not exploited as a source of energy. The aim is to change this. However, wind does have significant drawbacks as a source of energy because it is 'difficult to predict, intermittent, variable in strength, often there when not required and not there when required'.[5] The Spirit of Ireland initiative has provided a solution to these problems by proposing the construction of hydro-storage reservoirs in suitable mountain valleys, which would result in a cost-effective means of storing wind energy. This initiative promises to create thousands of jobs, reduce Ireland's carbon emissions, dramatically reduce Ireland's imported energy bill and basically solve a huge future energy problem for Ireland. In June 2009, I shared a podium with one of the drivers of this project at a business networking event and was blown away by the project. Provided the science stands up, and I am assured it does, this project has the potential to transform Ireland, and deserves political and popular support.

From where we stand at the moment, it is not clear where quality employment is going to come from in the Irish economy over the coming years, so it is imperative that our policy-makers create a plan outlining the sectors that offer longer-term potential, and then nurture an environment where these sectors can develop and prosper. I have identified some of the sectors that I believe represent the future of Ireland, but clearly areas relating to the so-called smart economy, research and development activities, and professional service exports will also have a key role to play in Ireland's future development. These sectors would support other activities, such as retail, financial services, the public sector and construction. Ireland also has a strong competitive advantage in music and the arts. These sectors should be encouraged to flourish and develop. The important point is that a more diversified economic base needs to be created, combining the modern with the traditional and the domestic with the foreign-owned. If we fail to adopt this more strategic approach, then Ireland will be stuck in a time warp of low quality employment, high unemployment, high levels of emigration and economic under-performance. Having had a taste of what is possible and having blown much of it away, it is now time to go back to the drawing board, learn lessons from past failures and get on with creating an alternative future.

9

Final Thoughts

The day is not far off when the economic problem will take the back seat where it belongs, and the arena of the heart and the head will be occupied, or reoccupied, by our real problems – the problems of life and of human relations, of creation and behaviour and religion.

John Maynard Keynes

This book was not intended as a re-writing of recent Irish history, but rather to give a personal perspective on where we have come from, what we have done wrong, the lessons that we must all learn and how we might plot the way forward. I am sure I will be criticised for dwelling too much on the past in this book, but I think it is important to understand how we got into this mess, learn the lessons, move on and never repeat our mistakes again.

The reality for Ireland is that, while we have become income rich over the past fifteen years, the country is still relatively new to the economic growth game and it has not been possible to build up the stock of public wealth that countries like Germany and France have. It takes generations of strong economic growth to build up public services and infrastructure, but unfortunately Ireland has now hit a severe speed wobble and there is a very real danger that some of the progress made could be reversed.

For those who have been around for long enough, in other words those who have lived through the dark and depressed

161

1980s, there is a real sense of déjà vu about where Ireland finds itself today. Like in the 1980s, unemployment is a major problem, the public finances are in serious trouble, emigration is becoming a necessity for some of our brightest and best young people, and there is a distinct lack of confidence in the ability of the political elite to address and sort out the numerous social and economic problems that are confronting the country. Be that as it may, it is important to recognise that an awful lot about life in Ireland today is better than it was in the 1980s, while accepting that some things are worse.

On the plus side, employment is twice as high today as in the 1980s, and young people have better access to all levels of education. The range of employment opportunity is also much broader than in the 1980s, notwithstanding the current difficulties in the labour market. The opportunity to travel abroad has never been better thanks to the revolution brought about by Michael O'Leary and Ryanair. There was a time when Aer Lingus enjoyed a total monopoly in Ireland and one almost had to take out a mortgage to fly to London. The boat was the only affordable way of getting off the island. Thankfully, the power of institutions such as the Church and the banks has been diminished. The choice and quality of food and restaurants is also immensely better today than in the 1980s, when an Indian curry or a Chinese takeaway were about as exotic as it got.

Despite the inadequacies of our road infrastructure, the situation is still a hell of a lot better today than it was. I have vivid memories of spending at least an hour caught in traffic in Naas every Friday evening on my way from Dublin to Waterford, and again in Kilcullen, Athy and Kilkenny. Back then, Irish motorists had a much more intimate knowledge of many towns and villages in Ireland than they would have desired, quite simply because they spent hours stuck in traffic in those towns and villages.

Although some things are undoubtedly better today than in the 1980s, many people are struggling to cope with the new economic and financial realities. This is because, after a period of such prosperity, our expectations are much higher and the majority of people have become used to a better standard of living than in the past. One thing that has surprised and, indeed, shocked me is the extent to which a lot of the apparent prosperity and bling evident over the past decade was driven by incredibly high levels of personal debt. This is now bearing down on the many people who are struggling to keep up with large mortgages, car loans and costs like private education. I have heard so many stories of ordinary families on relatively modest incomes who have borrowed aggressively for cars, houses and foreign holidays in recent years. This was sustainable as long as incomes were growing strongly and the labour market was performing well. With incomes now falling and thousands of jobs being lost, many ordinary families are in serious financial difficulty and it will take them a long time to recover. Brian Cowen[1] has argued that Ireland needs to accept a reduction of 10 per cent in living standards over the next two years, but unfortunately this will not be matched by a similar reduction in debt levels. This will be a difficult and painful reality for many people.

Two years ago I was standing in a line of people at a family wake in County Limerick, when a woman whom I had never seen before came up close to my face and called me a 'merchant of doom and gloom'. Perhaps she thought I was George Lee. Looking back on my commentary on the economy at the time, I was certainly not anything like as negative as I should have been, but it is very easy to analyse with the benefit of hindsight.

Throughout this book I have been extremely critical of the manner in which the Irish economy was managed or not managed between 1997 and 2008. Economic policy-making under Bertie Ahern has not been good for Ireland and undoubtedly created many of the problems with which we are now trying to grapple. Bertinomics is obviously not responsible for the global economic meltdown, but it certainly undermined the ability of the Irish economy to absorb and react to the global crisis. The manner in which public spending was allowed to escalate out of control, the failure to ensure value for money from all public spending, the inordinate dependence on the construction sector, the failure to regulate the banking system, and the pursuance of policies that basically blew the cost of living and the cost of doing business into the stratosphere all contributed to the eventual undoing of the Irish economic dream.

There has been a strong but disturbing tendency in Ireland over the past couple of years to bury the nation's collective head in the sand and not face up to the enormity of the problems that were clearly evolving in the economy. Unfortunately, this tendency was most pronounced amongst members of the Government and policy-makers in general, who took too long to realise the extent of the problems. By the time they did, it was too late and we have been running to catch up ever since.

Since the crisis erupted, public confidence has been extremely low. There is a strong feeling that we did not fully exploit the growth that was generated in the economy over the past decade and a half, and that many policy mistakes were made and a lot of money was wasted. In a crisis, be it in a family, a business or a country, a few ingredients are essential. First, the leader must give the impression of being in control, second, the leader must convince the people that there is a plan in place and, third, the leader must demonstrate that tough decisions will be taken to implement the plan. We may not like the medicine or agree with the plan, but at least strong, decisive leadership would inspire confidence. Such leadership has been sadly lacking in Ireland and the general population is not convinced that there is a credible plan in place; policy seems to be made up on the hoof. Perhaps that is not the reality, but it is the perception, and that perception has to change.

We must be careful, in a period of crisis like this, not to fall for some of the more radical left-wing solutions now being offered by some. The global capitalist system has not completely failed, but it has shown some significant flaws. With proper regulation and a more sensible approach to policy-making, it can be made to work again. Unfettered free market capitalism does not work, but neither does the opposite, as we found out in the past.

It is somewhat encouraging that, out of a sense of frustration, many private interests are becoming more proactive in trying to force the state structures to do the right things. Initiatives such as Spirit of Ireland, Emerge Ireland and the Ideas Campaign are all examples of private initiatives that are intent on creating a better future for Ireland. As citizens, we cannot stand back and hope that the state will solve all of our problems. We know from past experience that it won't. The diluted form of democracy in Ireland is first and foremost an impediment to the proper functioning of the state. Too many small vested interest groups have too much influence over key policy initiatives, thanks to the single transferable vote proportional representation electoral system. However, a fundamental restructuring of the electoral system is about as likely as a Waterford All-Ireland hurling victory.

Government has got to become more decisive in sorting out the obstacles to short-term economic recovery and longer-term economic prosperity. The key areas to be tackled are the banking system, the poor level of competitiveness in the economy and the structural imbalances in the public finances. Until all of these problems are sorted, it is hard to see any basis for recovery in the Irish economy. The social partnership model as currently constituted is not capable of solving the problems, and in my view is part of the problem rather than the solution. Crucially, powerful vested interest groups cannot be allowed to prevent the prosperous future that is possible, provided the correct policy decisions are pursued with a sense of urgency. Given the deep crisis the country now finds itself in, the time for prevarication is gone and the time for urgent action is now.

As a nation, we should expect a first-world health service, high quality public transport, high quality affordable housing, safe streets and an educational system that aspires to be amongst the best in the world. Our leaders owe it to us to map out where they want to take Ireland in the future.

Lessons must be learned from the mistakes of the past and a clear understanding developed of where growth in the Irish economy should come from in the future. We certainly sacrificed quality for quantity over the past decade. Quality has to become the byword of the future, in terms of quality of life and quality of economic growth. The fruits of future economic growth must not be wasted as in the past, but instead growth must be used to improve the quality of life of the population at large, and not just the few. Economic welfare is more important than economic growth and a society is more important than an economy, but the reality is that, without economic growth in the first place, it would be nearly impossible to generate economic welfare or to support society. However, the nature and quality of the economic growth and how its fruits are used are the most important considerations.

It angers me greatly that after a decade of such buoyant economic growth and revenue generation, Ireland is still left with a health service that doesn't know whether it is public or private, an education system that is under serious pressure and an IT infrastructure that is not quite in line with our claims to be a knowledge economy. On the plus side, the demise of the Celtic Tiger might just bring us back to earth and make us realise that the registrations of our cars, our addresses and our foreign holiday destinations are not what should define us as a people.

In 1930, John Maynard Keynes thought that richer societies would become more leisured ones, liberated from toil and hard work to enjoy the finer things in life. Yet, he discovered that they still work harder and harder to afford things that they believe will make them happy, only to discover those things don't make them happy. They also aspire to a higher status in society, but this forces others to run faster to keep up. In the end, everybody loses out; people have less leisure and pleasure in their lives. This aptly describes the rat race that the Irish were involved in over the past decade. We must now go back to first principles and start to appreciate the finer – and more simple – things in life.

Notes

Introduction

1 Allen, Kieran, *Ireland's Economic Crash: A Radical Agenda for Change*, Dublin: The Liffey Press, 2009.

Chapter 1

1 CSO.
2 CSO.
3 Department of the Environment, Heritage and Local Government.
4 CSO.
5 US Bureau of Economic Analysis.
6 Department of Finance.
7 CSO.
8 CSO.
9 CSO.
10 CSO.
11 IMF Country Report No.09/195, June 2009.
12 Statement by Brian Lenihan TD, Minister for Finance, 8 July 2008.
13 *Sunday Independent*, 15 March 2009.
14 Budget 2009, October 2008.
15 Department of Finance, Exchequer Returns 2008.
16 Statement by Brian Lenihan TD, Minister for Finance, 8 July 2008

Chapter 2
1 CSO.
2 Fianna Fáil Research and Support Services, briefing document, September 1976.
3 Fianna Fáil, 'Action Plan for National Reconstruction', General Election Manifesto 1977.
4 CSO.
5 CSO.
6 CSO.
7 McAleese, Dermot, 'Ireland's Economic Recovery', *Irish Banking Review*, Summer 1990.
8 CSO.
9 Department of Finance, *Budgetary and Economic Statistics*, September 2009; and my own estimates.
10 CSO.
11 CSO.
12 CSO.
13 CSO.

Chapter 3
1 United Nations, *Human Development Indices: A Statistical Update 2008*, United Nations Development Programme.
2 CSO.
3 CSO.
4 Corcoran, Jody, *Sunday Independent*, 23 August 2009.
5 CSO.

Chapter 4
1 Friends First, 'Quarterly Economic Outlook', November 2005.
2 DKM Economic Consultants, *Review of the Construction Industry 2007 and Outlook 2008–2010*, September 2008.
3 Department of Environment, Heritage and Local Government.
4 Office of the Revenue Commissioners.
5 Department of Finance and the Office of the Revenue Commissioners.
6 Central Bank of Ireland.
7 Bloomberg.
8 Bloomberg.
9 CSO.
10 CSO.
11 Central Bank of Ireland.

12 CSO.

13 Central Bank of Ireland.

14 Friends First, 'Are We Too Dependent on the Housing Market?', Quarterly Economic Outlook, March 2006.

15 CSO.

16 CSO.

17 CSO.

18 CSO.

19 CSO.

20 Central Bank of Ireland.

21 Central Bank of Ireland.

22 Department of Environment, Heritage and Local Government.

23 Irish Banking Federation.

24 Department of Environment, Heritage and Local Government.

25 Central Bank of Ireland.

26 Permanent TSB/ESRI.

27 Permanent TSB/ESRI.

28 Irish Banking Federation.

29 Department of Environment, Heritage and Local Government.

30 CSO.

Chapter 5

1 Office of the Revenue Commissioners and the CSO, *The Implications of Cross-Border Shopping for the Irish Exchequer*, Dublin, February 2009.

2 Eurostat, *Europe in Figures, Yearbook 2008*.

3 CSO and Eurostat.

4 CSO.

5 CSO.

6 Ahrend, Rudiger, Cournede, Boris and Price, Robert, 'Monetary Policy, Market Excesses and Financial Turmoil', OECD Working Paper No. 597, March 2008.

7 International Monetary Fund, *Staff Report for the 2009 Article IV Consultation with Ireland*, June 2009.

Chapter 6

1 Budget 2008.

2 Various national Budgets.

3 Department of Finance.

4 Department of Finance.

5 CSO, *Quarterly National Household Survey* (various).

6 Budget 2003.
7 *Quarterly National Household Survey*, September 2009.
8 CSO.
9 Cowen, Brian, 'The Bertie Years – Salute to the Celtic Tiger Taoiseach', *Irish Daily Star*, July 2008.
10 ESRI, *The Public–Private Sector Pay Gap in Ireland: What Lies Beneath*, October 2009.

Chapter 7
1 US Bureau of Economic Analysis.
2 *Sunday Tribune*, 'Top 50 AIB Customers Owe €19 Billion as Debts Escalate', 17 May 2009.
3 NCB Stockbrokers, *2020 Vision: Ireland's Demographic Dividend*, March 2006.
4 *Irish Times*, 'Reduced Demand Concerns Intel Staff', 20 July 2009.

Chapter 8
1 IDA Ireland, *Annual Report 2008*.
2 CSO and Forfás.
3 CSO.
4 National Competitiveness Council, *Annual Competitiveness Report 2008, Volume 1: Benchmarking Ireland's Performance*, 2009.
5 http://www.spiritofireland.org.

Chapter 9
1 *Irish Times*, 4 April 2009.

Index